# Japanese Folk Lore & Kami Traditions

## Sacred Spirits, Ancestral Beliefs, and Cultural Practices Rooted in Japanese Heritage

Akira Vale

# Table of Contents

Introduction ............................................................................. 1

Chapter 1: Where Spirit Meets Daily Life: Foundations of Kami Traditions ................................................................. 5

Chapter 2: The Landscape of Spirits: Nature, Place, and Sacred Presence ............................................................... 22

Chapter 3: Ancestral Ties: Households, Memory, and Everyday Reverence ............................................................ 37

Chapter 4: Seasons of Meaning: Calendars, Rites, and Agricultural Rhythms ......................................................... 53

Chapter 5: Tales with Teeth and Tails: Folklore as Cultural Code .......................................................................................... 70

Chapter 6: Signs and Gateways: Material Symbols of the Sacred ........................................................................................ 86

Chapter 7: Performance and Procession: Movement as Story ........................................................................................... 101

Chapter 8: Blended Paths: Syncretism, Doctrine, and Local Practice ...................................................................................... 116

Chapter 9: Local Worlds: Regions, Crafts, and Story-Places ................................................................................................. 132

Chapter 10: Continuity and Change: Modern Encounters with the Sacred ..................................................................... 147

Conclusion ........................................................................ 163

Reference List .................................................................. 167

# Introduction

At sunrise in a quiet Kyoto neighborhood, a single mother stands at her front door, straightening the shimenawa—twisted straw rope—she made with her daughter for New Year's. She pours a small cup of water onto the step, not out of habit, but as a gentle greeting to the unseen guests she feels moving through their home. Across the city, elders sweep shrine paths while children flutter between festival stalls, pausing to clap twice before an ancient camphor tree wrapped in zigzag paper. In these moments, the ordinary is anything but: every gesture, every shared glance, becomes a thread that ties people to hidden presences, family, and place. Japanese folk spirituality lives here—in small acts, seasons turning, and stories told over breakfast—quietly shaping meaning long after ceremonies end.

Maybe you've found yourself wondering: What does it really mean to believe in kami? Is this about worshipping distant gods, or is it about noticing the presence of something sacred in daily life—the light on a garden stone, the hush before a festival dance? How do rituals and symbols actually work in the rhythms of home and community? And most importantly, how can someone appreciate or participate in these traditions in a way that feels respectful, authentic, and free from the anxieties of cultural missteps?

Introduction

This book is here for those questions. It aims to offer more than lists of customs or museum quotes—it's a guide into the living heart of Japanese folk spirituality. Through vivid stories, careful research, and honest conversation, you'll discover how communities make sense of spiritual presence, why simple objects hold so much power, and how everyday acts become vessels for memory and trust. Along the way, you'll gain tools to untangle the meanings behind household altars, village festivals, and guardian trees—not just as a visitor or admirer, but as someone ready to form deeper, more thoughtful connections across culture and time.

Many of us arrive at topics like these with a mix of excitement and caution. Maybe you've flipped through shallow guides or seen flashy travel snaps that reduce centuries of tradition to hashtags and souvenirs. You might worry about romanticizing the past, or worse, accidentally appropriating what isn't yours to claim. These are real concerns. This book invites you to navigate them with care. Every page is shaped by a belief that true appreciation starts with listening, questioning assumptions, and honoring complexity. Here, there are no perfect experts—just fellow travelers, learning to move gently through unfamiliar worlds.

Why trust this journey? The path you're about to follow is traced by someone who has spent years both studying and illustrating Japanese folklore, blending anthropological insight with a love of visual storytelling. My background weaves together archival research, fieldwork in rural and urban Japan, and close collaborations with tradition bearers. Whether drawing festival dancers, transcribing stories from elders, or restoring old ema and amulets, I bring a commitment to telling stories that are as nuanced as they are beautiful. The result is a narrative rich with scenes, voices, and images—one that honors complexity and never flattens the lived experience of real people.

The chapters ahead are designed as a guided journey. We begin where spirit meets daily life—with the foundational habits and memories that anchor belief, before wandering through mountains, rivers, and sacred groves where nature pulses with presence. From there, you'll enter households where ancestor tablets glow, witness how storytelling passes ethics through generations, and see how seemingly simple objects—ropes, bells, charms—carry layers of ritual and emotion. Performance and craft, mixed traditions, regional flavors, and modern adaptations each have their place, woven together with reflection and visual cues. Each theme builds on the last, leading you from first encounters to contemporary questions about continuity, change, and personal engagement. Throughout, sidebars and glossaries provide context without interrupting the story's flow, ensuring clarity even when the language grows poetic or layered.

You don't need specialized knowledge or formal training to begin—just a spirit of curiosity and openness. The tone throughout is warm, conversational, and sometimes playful, modeling the very humility and presence that define much of Japanese folk practice. Consider this introduction your invitation to set aside preconceptions, to let metaphor and memory guide you, and to savor the slow unfolding of meaning chapter by chapter.

## Introduction

So, welcome. You're about to cross a threshold—into a world alive with stories, gestures, and the gentle murmur of spirit in unexpected places. Read on with open senses: let yourself be surprised, moved, and challenged. May this book offer not only knowledge, but also a new way of seeing: one where myth shapes memory, where care transforms the everyday, and where belonging starts with attentive wonder. Let's begin.

# Chapter 1: Where Spirit Meets Daily Life: Foundations of Kami Traditions

Imagine you have a small garden where every decision about planting, watering, and care changes how well your plants grow over the season. Now, think of your life as this garden, with daily choices acting like different ways to invest time and attention. Just as some investment approaches might lead to steady growth while others take bigger risks for potentially larger rewards, the way people in traditional Japan approached the presence of kami influenced their everyday lives and long-term well-being. These strategies weren't written down in formal rules but were learned through observation, memory, and a deep sense of connection to the world around them.

This chapter invites you into that world, where spiritual presence meets daily practice. You'll see how communities balanced hope and care, using rituals, stories, and simple gestures to nurture relationships with the unseen forces woven into nature and human experience. By exploring these living traditions, we can better understand how ordinary moments become sacred touchpoints, shaping not just beliefs but how life unfolds from dawn's first sweep of the threshold to the shared rhythms of festival and harvest.

## Kami Traditions Explained

To understand how presence shaped ordinary behavior, we begin with what 'kami' meant to those whose lives unfolded within this worldview. In old Japan, animism was a lived reality rather than an abstract label. People looked at the world around them—waterfalls roaring down cliffs, pines twisted by wind, even the well in the backyard—and felt something more than inanimate matter. These things could become *kami*, but not because of formal belief or fixed doctrine. Presence mattered; people paid attention at certain moments—a hush before entering a forest path, a whispered greeting to the one-legged Jizō statue by a stream. Encounters happened where change pressed close: thresholds between house and street, spring's first thaw, the day of harvest. Kami were met through relationship and outcome: if a spring gave clean water each year, kindness was returned with offerings. If an illness faded after prayers at a mossed stone, the place became special. Fertility, protection, and purification were known in events: the fields yielding abundance, safe returns from distant rivers, health restored after ritual cleansing (Shinto, Nature and Ideology in Contemporary Japan: Making Sacred Forests 1474289932, 9781474289931, n.d.). These presences weren't confined to dramatic natural landmarks—they flowed into everyday and seasonal rhythms, shaping how people moved, greeted, and cared for their surroundings.

Everyday sacredness wove itself into routine. Each morning, you might sweep the threshold—not only to clear dust, but in careful strokes that honored unseen guests. Hanging first-picked fruit on a small shelf in the kitchen wasn't a ritual separate from making breakfast; it was part of greeting the day, as much habit as devotion. When a child was born or named, neighbors would gather, timing celebrations with the village's festival calendar so that private milestones threaded into shared cycles of planting and thanksgiving. Shrine visits marked the start of rice-planting, coming-of-age, and memorial passages, keeping personal life in step with community time (Fujiwara & Miura, 2025). Days had texture: some were more auspicious, others avoided for journeys or new projects. None of these choices followed strict rules handed down from authority. Instead, local memory and advice—shared over meals or in stories—taught which hillsides sheltered kind spirits and when a door should remain shut at dusk. This approach didn't divide "work" from "worship." Reverence and necessity walked side by side, letting spiritual care feel as familiar as tending a garden or minding a fire.

Village tradition came before religious institution. Local elders, families, or even select individuals managed the care of simple shrines and scheduled festivals, following guidance shaped by nature, season, and communal need (Shinto, Nature and Ideology In Contemporary Japan: Making Sacred Forests 1474289932, 9781474289931, n.d.). In coastal areas, fishermen offered thanks for safe passage, while in mountain hamlets, caretakers watched springs and sacred stones, marking boundaries with ropes or planted saplings. As time passed, larger structures and state involvement layered new forms onto these old roots. Standardization brought uniform rituals, priestly lineages, and national shrine connections. Even so, the shape of worship held onto local flavor: song dialects, homegrown dances, and unique offerings survived alongside official ceremonies. This variety is important because institutions like modern Shinto represent only one expression among many. Earlier folkways—sometimes called shrine-centered religion, sometimes simply "the ways of the kami"—remained flexible, adapting to outside influence but never fully erased. These traditions later intertwined, sometimes uneasily, with Buddhist temples and the policies of rulers, a theme we'll encounter again (Fujiwara & Miura, 2025). Understanding all this means listening to the words people used and noticing what slips between lines when we try to tidy things up with categories.

Some ideas do not fit neatly into English. *Kami* points to what inspires awe—mountains shrouded in mist, ancestors who linger, field markers worn smooth by generations. It doesn't just mean "god" or "spirit," but signals presence across a wide range of beings and phenomena, always felt rather than simply classified. Another word, *musubi*, hints at connection and creative power: the way life binds together in growth, weaving root to leaf, parent to child, season to renewal (Shinto, Nature and Ideology in Contemporary Japan: Making Sacred Forests 1474289932, 9781474289931, n.d.). Trying to translate these terms with a single definition flattens their meaning. Better to hold them lightly, as metaphors or patterns that reveal themselves through stories, songs, or quiet acts. This book uses examples and context to open such concepts, building depth as we move forward. With these guides in mind, we can now see how relationships with kami took form—in village shrines, roadside markers, and the edges of groves where pathways slipped from everyday into extraordinary.

## From Village Shrines to Living Heritage

These kami presences we've been discussing didn't remain abstract—they anchored themselves in specific places where daily life and spiritual attention met. The breath of the sacred could be felt not only in forest groves or mountain mists but also beside a simple wooden gate, at a crossroads, or near a cold stream running behind rice fields. Village shrines emerged as the everyday meeting grounds between invisible blessing and concrete survival needs, making the presence of kami tangible for everyone who passed by.

**Tutelary Roots**

Walking along earthen paths skirting freshly planted paddies, it is easy to imagine the fraught balance villagers once navigated between hope and hardship. Boundary markers— whether upright stones or humble straw ropes—did more than separate properties; they summoned tutelary presences believed to regulate peace and plenty. Settling a dispute over whose rows belonged where was rarely just about lines drawn in mud. These negotiations unfolded under the silent gaze of field guardians, their sites thick with generations of whispered petitions: please spare us drought, keep pests away, protect our shared water.

Riverside altars made of stacked rocks often held a ladle or bowl for offerings left by those drawing water. These were tokens of respect for the river's dual gift and threat—life flowing for crops, floods looming after storms. In mountain passes, travelers knelt before weathered statues or twisted branches, hoping for clear skies, safe passage, and goodwill from both human neighbors and local spirits. Even bridges took on extra meaning: stone foxes or masked figures stood watch, reminding all that moving across water meant entering another space, subject to new possibilities or dangers.

Shrines didn't just support agriculture. They watched over market days, childbirths, newcomer arrivals, and seasonal illnesses. Each place where people lingered, worried, or hoped might call for its own small sanctuary. Whether placed atop village hills or tucked against merchant rows, these shrines suited their settings and practical needs, folding the sacred into the most ordinary moments (Banda et al., 2024).

**Ritual Calendars**

The seasons pressed themselves into every layer of community life, and shrine rituals offered a shared way to read and respond to those cycles. Planting ceremonies often involved gathering beneath blossoming trees to offer rice cakes or sake, asking the kami for gentle rains and mild winds—conditions that impacted not just yields but whether a family ate well come autumn. Thunder drums echoed across villages as protection prayers during typhoon season, blending meteorological anxiety with spiritual hope. When harvest arrived, thankfulness spilled into festivals marked by singing, drumming, and food sharing. These were more than celebrations; they served as practical systems for redistributing grain or vegetables, supporting families hit by poor yields and tightening the social weave.

New Year purification rituals set a distinct rhythm, pausing daily toil so people could sweep away old troubles, cleanse household tools, and refresh bonds with both ancestors and neighbors. Over time, patterns like sowing, reaping, and resting became encoded in local calendars that interwove agricultural cycles with communal moral practice. Cold snaps or dry spells brought extra prayers, while bountiful years inspired added dances and feasts. This wasn't simply custom; it was an ecological conversation, shaped by observation and memory, a living record of adapting to climate chances and misfortunes (Banda et al., 2024; *Explore the Fascinating Realm of Ancient History - Scripture Analysis*, 2025).

**Story as Charter**

Every shrine carried a founding story—tales that explained not only why an altar stood in one spot, but what it should receive in return. These stories acted as charters, authorizing local practice and rooting people's behavior in something larger. Perhaps a deity appeared to someone in a dream, instructing them to stack stones beside a gushing spring; maybe a serpent revealed itself at planting time, blessing the earth if fed first fruits. Where stories flourished, landscape and belief grew together, each spring or hilltop carrying a memory that guided how—and why—villagers approached certain places or left particular gifts. If one shrine demanded rice cakes in autumn but another called for wildflowers in spring, origin tales preserved those differences, explaining them and reinforcing kinship among community, land, and ancestral spirit. Local legends kept ethics close to home, showing that right relationship with the unseen world required attentiveness, humility, and care (*Explore the Fascinating Realm of Ancient History – Scripture Analysis*, 2025).

**Continuity Through Change**

As cities swelled and Japan's religious landscape shifted—sometimes pulled toward Buddhist customs, sometimes nudged by government reform—village shrines adapted. Some moved or rebuilt as rice fields turned into neighborhoods, though their protective function stayed constant. Others found fresh meaning as cultural heritage sites, taking on new roles as places for neighborhood meetings or children's games. Even when state policies tried separating shrine and temple, syncretic practices persisted quietly; incense or scripture readings might blend with local rites. What mattered most was that these spaces continued to anchor community need: distributing food after storms, storing festival decorations, serving as safe harbors in uncertain times (Banda et al., 2024).

Heritage efforts today build on this long lineage, working not only to preserve architecture but to sustain the choices, gestures, and responsibilities that make shrines living sites of belonging (Banda et al., 2024). Even when labeled as culture more than faith, these places echo with the work of caretakers, storytellers, and volunteers—people who tend altars, mend fences, or organize processions. In this way, village shrines show how adaptation can nurture continuity, keeping ties strong across both celebration and crisis.

What endures above all are the stories—carried in conversations, retold through dance or painted banners—that breathe life into these spaces. Shrines persevere when communities remember not just the rules, but the reasons for reverence. Before turning to the art of telling and interpreting these stories, we pause at the threshold, recognizing how memory and meaning have always traveled hand-in-hand from holy ground to hearth.

## Storytelling as Cultural Memory

These sacred sites and seasonal rhythms didn't persist through written doctrine alone—they lived in the tales grandmothers told at winter hearths and the songs farmers sang at planting time. The true breath of kami traditions moved through story, not only stone or ceremony—folktales were practical cultural technologies, memory-systems alive in everyday lives. Each fable, song, and whispered legend worked as a social blueprint, preserving values, explaining landscapes, and guiding behavior without reliance on formal instruction or printed texts.

Stories passed by word of mouth had to be easy to recall and quick to retell. Short motifs like foxes, cranes, or river spirits became memory anchors that helped listeners carry crucial lessons from one generation to the next. For example, children heard over and over how a fox spirit might reward honesty but punish liars with mischief or loss, making the risks of deceit feel immediate and personal. During rice planting, workers might sing refrains reminding them of reciprocity rules—never take without giving, never boast of what is borrowed. These ritual cues often slid naturally into the actions people performed; bowing at a torii (a sacred gate) before entering woods or refusing to cross a boundary marked with shimenawa (twisted straw rope signaling sacred ground) became scripts learned through narrative, rather than dictated law. Stories functioned as cultural survival tools, encoding social guidelines in characters and actions impossible to forget.

Tales also knitted together community memory by tying values to visible places. Each cedar draped with shimenawa, each spring named for a spirit's visit, stood as a living textbook. A grandmother might point to a mossy stone and recount how a kami disguised as a traveler rested there and blessed the village after being given water. That story turned the rock from an anonymous object into a sacred reference point: a child grew up knowing this was not just any stone, but 'the Traveler's Stone,' carrying both warning and encouragement for those who passed. Similar stories explained which mountain paths were safe, which should be avoided, or how to greet local spirits encountered during seasonal rituals. Land itself became a map traced in legend—travelers remembered routes by the tales linked to every bend and bridge, villages carried their own micro-geographies of memory that linked story and place so closely they could not be separated.

The heart of many of these narratives lay in the roles inhabited by tricksters, helpers, and guardians. Tricksters like kitsune and tanuki exposed greed or pride, not by outright shaming, but by turning foolishness into laughter and gentle warning. Many stories show villagers learning humility when outwitted by a clever animal—teaching that self-importance leads to trouble, while those who help others (be it a wounded crane or lost traveler) receive kindness in return. Guardian spirits enforced boundaries through story: polluting a river might bring bad luck, or failing to keep a promise would lead to direct consequences—a hint that breaking trust, even unseen, upset the balance of daily life. Stories rarely offered simple heroes or villains. Spirits could be dangerous or generous, depending on context, teaching listeners to watch carefully and act thoughtfully in a world where intentions matter as much as actions. One well-known folk story tells of a tanuki who tricks a greedy merchant, only for the tanuki to be caught and then released by a kind farmer—the lesson lands gently but firmly: generosity and discernment build lasting harmony.

Oral tradition kept these tales alive, shaping new versions as times changed. Storytellers updated details to fit changing circumstances: the mountain trail became a train route, the riverbank a city canal, yet the story's lesson about caring for place and neighbor passed unchanged. Schoolchildren might act out ancient legends at festivals, or families gather to hear a tale in which an old drum is replaced by a radio, showing how modern elements join time-honored themes. While some stories entered books or national celebrations, local variations persisted in home kitchens and neighborhood streets, adapting to new challenges while holding onto the core. Oral tradition spun a living web—old wisdom, ready for today.

This capacity for adaptation gives oral storytelling a power beyond passive memory. Folktales taught people not only what to remember, but how to respond to change—offering tools for resilience and ethical choice. Understanding how these tales functioned in their original communities—as teaching tools, memory aids, and moral frameworks—prepares us to approach them with the care and context they deserve, rather than extracting them as spiritual techniques for personal use. In telling and listening with respect for context, readers begin to glimpse the living heart of kami tradition.

# Reading Without Ritual Prescription

As we saw in the previous section, Japanese folktales and rituals carry memory; they hold stories of grandparents, village struggles, seasonal hopes, and local spirits. These aren't just tales for entertainment or instructions to copy at home but are ways a community records its dreams and losses. When you approach these living traditions, interpretive humility is your first tool. Instead of asking, "How can I use this ritual?" start with, "What did this mean for those who gathered here?" Imagine visiting a friend's home: you don't rearrange framed family pictures, but you might ask about them, listen, and learn the stories behind each moment. In the same way, seeking voices from within—through interviews, museum captions, or firsthand accounts—helps you discover what questions are welcome and which themes are better left as quiet observation (*An Annotated Bibliography of Global and Non-Western Rhetorics: Sources for Comparative Rhetorical Studies – Present Tense*, n.d.).

Context shapes everything in folk practice. Before reading a story or describing a ritual, it helps to pause and imagine its setting. Was this a fishing village where sea dangers shaped beliefs? Or a mountain hamlet where landslides threatened crops? A thick braided rope strung across a mountain path isn't just a symbol—it might be a protection against both physical risk and spiritual impurity. In the same way, ringing a temple bell means something different during a New Year festival than during a local wedding. Try comparing gestures and customs across regions: do two towns share the same way of welcoming spirits, or does one add a touch borrowed from distant mountain lore? This approach keeps interpretations grounded, preventing the temptation to flatten every ritual into the same meaning.

When you read words like "kami," "musubi," or "harai," there is no single dictionary answer. "Kami" could be a waterfall spirit, an ancestor believed to protect the family, or a fox bringing messages from the unseen world. Context changes everything—just as sunlight makes a cloth appear blue at noon and gray at dusk. Consulting different translations, pausing over footnotes, or rereading a phrase in context lets you notice these color shifts. For example, one storyteller may call a river-kami playful, while another describes the same kami as fierce when storms threaten the village. Checking side-by-side versions of old tales, or looking up regional terms, helps you see how a word lives differently in each story.

Source awareness sits at the heart of respectful engagement. Every account comes from somewhere—from a grandmother at the hearth, a city government pamphlet, or a tourist booklet meant for visitors. The tone and intent change accordingly. A government festival guide might list only appealing highlights, while family memories add personal names and minor details outsiders rarely hear. In tourism brochures, rituals can be simplified or made more dramatic. Try reading the same festival's description on a city website and then in a neighbor's recollection: new layers of meaning will stand out. Stories also reshape themselves depending on the audience, just as the tales adults tell children on holidays differ from those retold for local pride or written for movie scripts (*Localizing the Global: The Shakuhachi's Place in "American" Culture - ProQuest*, 2022). Recognizing these filters lets you tread softly, aware that every retelling shapes what is visible—and what remains hidden.

These strategies prepare you for upcoming chapters exploring sacred woods, family altars, and lively festivals. The careful habits described here—humility, context, language care, and source awareness—aren't skills to perfect once and set aside but practical tools you'll reach for often. They help you avoid forcing square pegs into round holes, creating space for lively traditions to speak on their own terms instead of becoming extensions of what is already familiar (*An Annotated Bibliography of Global and Non-Western Rhetorics: Sources for Comparative Rhetorical Studies – Present Tense*, n.d.). As you move forward, keep adding to your interpretive toolkit, ready to meet each story, site, or song with curiosity rather than prescription.

*Interpretive Toolkit Checklist*

- Begin with questions about meaning for the original community, not personal benefit
- Zoom out: consider setting, season, and social backdrop before interpreting symbols
- Approach language as shifting and multicolored—check multiple translations if possible

- Identify sources and understand their intent (local, academic, promotional)
- Notice differences in how stories are told for locals, children, or outsiders
- Stay open to being corrected by those with direct experience
- Keep notes on shifts in word use, symbolism, and presentation

Use this checklist as you continue through stories, landscapes, and rituals ahead. Each habit grows with practice and makes room for genuine understanding.

## Bringing It All Together

Throughout this chapter, we've explored how the idea of kami shaped daily life in Japanese villages—not as distant spirits but as part of every morning routine, seasonal ritual, and story passed from one generation to the next. We saw that shrines weren't just religious buildings; they were meeting points where community needs and spiritual care blended together. Traditions grew out of lived experiences, guided by the changing rhythms of nature, local memory, and acts of kindness or respect for the world around them. The stories, songs, and small gestures people carried into their daily lives gave presence to kami and kept these connections alive across centuries.

As you move forward, it's important to remember that these traditions are not only about ceremony or belief—they're about building meaningful relationships with place, people, and history. Stories helped communities adapt and stay resilient through change, and rituals made everyday actions more thoughtful and connected. By looking closely at language, context, and sources, we learn to approach these living practices with humility and care, rather than trying to fit them into set categories or quick explanations. This awareness opens us up to a deeper appreciation of Japanese folk spirituality, reminding us that real understanding starts with curiosity, respect, and a willingness to see the world through many different eyes.

## Chapter 2: The Landscape of Spirits: Nature, Place, and Sacred Presence

When a mountain is reduced to lines on a map showing height and slope, what stories vanish? The fierce weather that gathers on its broad shoulders, the rivers that begin their journeys from its snowmelt, the worn paths where ancestors once walked just to greet the breaking dawn—all these are missing. Think about a river: it doesn't simply carve out land or carry water; it's believed to wash away impurities, but might it also carry tales, emotions, and memories from one life shore to another? And consider an ancient cedar wrapped in a thick straw rope—does that rope only shield the tree, or does it also shape how we see and honor the world through this living presence?

Think for a moment about your own favorite place—a park, a garden, or a quiet street corner—that makes you slow down, change your mood, or whisper to yourself without any signs telling you how to behave. Now imagine an entire culture where such places don't just exist quietly; instead, they speak back, shaping how people move, think, and connect each day. This chapter invites you to explore how mountains, rivers, and trees are not mere landscapes but living companions with moods and voices in Japanese spirituality. They call for respect, attentiveness, and understanding, revealing a world where nature and spirit are deeply entwined and ever-present.

## Mountains, Rivers, and Trees as Living Presences

In Chapter 1, kami presence was shown shaping daily rhythms across village life; now attention settles on the landforms where this presence gathers most vividly. Mountains, rivers, trees, stones, and springs are not passive backdrops in Japanese folk spirituality but felt as living neighbors. Each has its own moods, influences, and expectations. These natural features become centers of spiritual activity, where the boundary between visible and invisible is most permeable.

Mountains rise behind villages, drawing clouds, catching rain, releasing springs that feed rice fields and homes. Their shapes make wind patterns, their slopes gather snow, and their creeks sing through every season. People notice these changes. When a mountain's first cap of snow appears, elders might advise on when to plant winter vegetables or warn young people against climbing too high out of respect for nesting birds. In some areas, the harvest festival is tied directly to the arrival of fresh water from mountain melt, honoring the peak's steady generosity. Climbing a mountain for pilgrimage is less an act of conquering and more a careful approach: each step upwards is both a physical challenge and a patterned gesture of readiness. The body strains, breathes harder, and with each

## Chapter 2: The Landscape of Spirits: Nature, Place, and Sacred Presence

turn in the path, ordinary conversation fades, replaced by quiet focus. These practices do not treat mountains as abstract symbols but as immediate providers and vigilant observers—participants in local life. Later in Chapter 9, you'll see how these relationships change from region to region, sometimes mapping entire networks of sacred paths and annual circuits.

Rivers move differently. They do not just mark where one field ends and another begins. Their flows are watched for signs of flood or drought, but also for opportunities to reset and cross thresholds. Ritual washing at a riverbank before shrine visits isn't only about getting clean—it's an act of letting moving water carry away what needs to be left behind. Feet cleansed, worries washed off, one is ready to meet the sacred with fewer burdens. At crossings, it's common to see travelers pause, bow, or leave a coin near the foot of a bridge post. Families visiting relatives may stop at a ford and quietly offer thanks for a safe passage, trusting that the flow recognizes both departure and return. Where two streams meet, people sometimes choose these places for vows or farewells, feeling that confluences hold special power: the joining or parting of currents stands in for the choices and journeys in human lives. These actions show how rivers aren't simply water channels—they are participants in important turning points, boundary-keepers that must be acknowledged.

Aged trees pull attention almost effortlessly. When a trunk stretches thick and roots break through stone, someone will tie a braided straw rope—shimenawa—around its base. White zigzag paper shide flutter from these ropes, setting off a space to approach carefully. Village gatherings often center beneath broad canopies, stringing festival decorations or posting notices on wooden boards attached to the tree. Over years, certain hollows become places for quiet prayers, while children are taught to lower their voices and bow before passing. If damage comes—a broken branch, graffiti scar—it is not only environmental harm but a violation of mutual trust between people and what dwells here. A village elder may tell younger generations why New Year decorations belong only on a specific cedar, linking stories to the visible form. Across seasons, the same tree stands as witness, collecting memories in rings and bark, anchoring community life and spiritual expectation. In Chapter 4, how festivals reawaken these sites becomes a central theme.

Stones and springs hold attention through their presence and feel. An oddly shaped boulder along a path, smoothed by years of hands brushing its side, draws small offerings: a pinch of salt, rice grains resting on its surface. Springs are approached with measured steps; ladles rest nearby for those who wish to wash hands, cool faces, or fill containers. Pathways bend slightly so as not to confront a stone too directly, marking respect through action rather than signposts. Cold, clear spring water on palms, the ache of dipped fingers in winter, the stony weight of a balanced rock after rainfall—all create moments when the senses sharpen, making the invisible feel close. The etiquette around these places formalizes gratitude: never taking more than you need, pausing even when hurried, remembering to look down and acknowledge what steadies your day. Such behavior echoes practices among animist societies worldwide, where certain locations gain memory, wisdom, and spirit (Swancutt, 2019).

Having recognized how distinct landforms shape behavior and meaning, the next section broadens the view to a world suffused with countless presences.

## The Ten Thousand Kami Idea

Having explored how mountains, rivers, groves, and stones come alive in Japanese belief, it helps to step back and see the wider view that shapes these encounters. In this worldview, spirits are not rare guests—everywhere, presences flicker just out of sight. People describe this as "yaoyorozu-no-kami," meaning "eight million kami" or, less literally, "ten thousand kami." The number hints at an abundance too great to count, a poetic reminder that sacred presence has no finish line (*Shinto: Kami, Nature Spirits & Ancestors | Asian Gods and Goddesses Class Notes*, 2025). This approach does not map out a closed pantheon like Greek or Norse mythology. Instead, every place, thing, or even event might be recognized as carrying its own spirit, with room for both heritage and surprise.

Walking in an old village, a person might pause at a bend in a path where the wind always feels different, or notice a loom that has lasted through three generations. Over time, the community may treat that spot or object with gentle care, telling stories about the quiet presence they sense there. That respected loom sometimes becomes more than a tool; it earns offerings of rice or flowers, a bow before use, or even a small plaque if it finally retires. On a busy street, a rough but resilient stone could draw small tokens from passersby who believe it watches travelers. These recognitions vary by region and family, reflecting the flexible nature of the yaoyorozu-no-kami idea while tying people to shared ways of honoring what endures beyond ordinary sight (*Shinto: Kami, Nature Spirits & Ancestors | Asian Gods and Goddesses Class Notes*, 2025).

This web of reverence also shapes daily habits and ethical choices. Courtesy extends beyond people to things and places. Before stepping through a torii—a bright gate marking the edge of sacred space—visitors pause for a shallow bow, acknowledging the territory of unseen company. At shrines, a simple ritual unfolds: hands and mouths are rinsed with fresh water, symbolizing a wish to clear away dust and muddle that might block healthy relationships with both humans and spirits. Some quietly offer thanks beside an ancient tree or leave small gifts near a flowing spring. Even cleaning becomes more than a chore; during seasons like New Year's, families sweep and tidy their homes to express gratitude to spaces that shelter them and to keep a good relationship with household spirits (*Shinto: Kami, Nature Spirits & Ancestors | Asian Gods and Goddesses Class Notes*, 2025).

Care also appears in the way everyday objects are handled. Tools passed down generations often receive careful storage and respectful use, as though the effort spent polishing a blade or folding away a garment returns thanks for loyal service. When tools reach the end of usefulness, some households hold a tiny ceremony to rest the object and invite its spirit to find peace. Through these gestures, communities nurture mindfulness, discouraging waste, and remembering that attention is a kind of offering. Children learn early that a casual toss or harsh word toward belongings can feel like an insult to silent companions. This ethic works quietly, blending gratitude and restraint into the rhythm of ordinary life (*Shinto: Kami, Nature Spirits & Ancestors | Asian Gods and Goddesses Class Notes*, 2025).

Places do not belong to just one presence. A single shrine or grove might host a guardian kami, ancestral spirits, and nature-aligned presences together, each with special responsibilities. One celebration honors the local harvest and invites blessing for rice fields. Another calls on storm gods to protect against summer lightning. Later in the year, rituals ask spirits to keep roads safe or shield villagers from illness. Each role layers atop the others, shaped by custom, season, and storytelling. Communities negotiate which aspect receives focus—not through rivalry, but by weaving needs and histories into a living pattern. This approach means contradiction rarely troubles anyone; instead, flexibility and shared care stand out. Where some Western traditions seek tidy exclusivity, Shinto sees multiple powers thriving side by side, turning diversity into harmony (*Shinto: Kami, Nature Spirits & Ancestors | Asian Gods and Goddesses Class Notes*, 2025).

The most visible signs of respect for this animating network are in posture, movement, and voice. Visitors to sacred sites often move quietly, walk with gentle steps, and use hushed voices, sending a message of shared presence rather than self-importance. Bowing at the threshold of a grove or near a shrine gate marks entering a shared world, asking permission rather than claiming. Water rinses hands and lips, clearing pathways for clean intention. These gestures are not tests of belief but invitations to pause, observe, and recognize another way of being. For those aiming to honor Japanese practice, watching with care and learning the meaning behind these acts expresses understanding and appreciation without crossing lines into imitation (*Shinto: Kami, Nature Spirits & Ancestors | Asian Gods and Goddesses Class Notes*, 2025).

All of these ideas and behaviors focus with special intensity at the edge of chinju no mori—sacred groves where boundaries between worlds feel softest and the presence of many kami is felt in the hush beneath ancient trees. In approaching these living thresholds, the philosophy of the ten thousand kami takes shape you can almost touch.

## Chinju no Mori: Sacred Grove Logic

This sensibility of presence everywhere finds one of its most deliberate expressions in the chinju no mori, or shrine grove. Walking toward a Shinto shrine, a visitor often notices a gradual shift in air and atmosphere. The temperature dips beneath dense leaves, sunlight filters softly, and stone paths narrow under the weight of time and footsteps. Stepping onto moss-laced ground, the shift is both physical and mental—a pause that signals entry into a different order of space. These groves function as intentional buffers where the everyday world recedes and attentiveness grows sharper. Even before reading a sign or seeing a torii gate, the senses mark this as a threshold, a living boundary between lived human space and the realm where kami—spirit presences—are not just possible but expected. In this way, chinju no mori turns abstract belief into walkable form, using landscape itself to tune people's awareness (Sustainability Directory, 2025).

Within the shade of these groves, memory gathers in both bark and story. Elder trees stand as living records, their rings keeping track of centuries just as local tales attach names and histories to roots and clearings. An ancient cedar might host offerings in its hollow, while another patch preserves rare understory plants that have survived waves of change outside the grove. Landmarks within chinju no mori, such as a particular boulder or a spring, are woven with stories of past festivals, founding deities, or even historical crises. At the turn of each season, community members gather for rites that double as ecological upkeep—sweeping fallen leaves, renewing talismans, tending to signs of animal burrows. Conservation here is not an act apart from tradition; it is the ongoing rehearsal of remembrance, where protecting habitat means keeping shared stories alive together (Sustainability Directory, 2025).

Sound shapes experience in ways as textured as sight. Inside a chinju no mori, the usual thrum of town life falls away behind layers of leaf and air. Moss muffles steps. A breeze overhead may set bamboo to whisper. Birds offer clear notes, their calls echoing through filtered sunlight. In these moments, silence reveals itself as full rather than empty: every hush contains a potential for encounter. To gently break this quiet, shrines sometimes hang small bells, wind chimes, or wooden clappers near entrances or sacred trees. The focused ring draws attention without shouting, inviting visitors to notice how all their senses are involved in meeting the sacred. This orchestration of stillness and careful sound becomes a way for the unseen presences to be felt through listening as much as looking. The land teaches patience and presence, hinting at mysteries worth waiting to perceive (Sustainability Directory, 2025).

Caring for a grove is an act carried forward by neighbors, elders, and children alike. Volunteer days follow a rhythm of shared labor: trimming pathways, repairing ropes around protected trunks, sometimes sharing food and stories after the work is done. The rules that guide conduct—no taking wood, no littering, quiet voices—are heard less as imposed restrictions and more as gestures of gratitude and belonging. These limits arise naturally from the sense that the grove is both ancestor and neighbor, worthy of respect simply by being there. Offering donations or participating in seasonal festivals is understood not only as shrine support but also as investment in living heritage and habitat health. As each person helps shape the grove's future, they become part of a chain of care stretching across generations. Having crossed the grove threshold, we can read the material signs—ropes, stories, wooden tablets—that guide conduct within and around sacred spaces, learning what it means for a place to "speak back" and shape our everyday choices (Sustainability Directory, 2025).

Chapter 2: The Landscape of Spirits: Nature, Place, and Sacred Presence

# Markers of Presence: Rocks, Ropes, and Signs

Having crossed the grove threshold, a visitor finds the landscape changing not just in mood but in detail. The stones and lanterns that mark these spaces set a pattern for the movement ahead. Touching the world lightly, they guide attention toward unseen presences. Material markers—ropes, rocks, signs—make the invisible readable and teach how to step forward with care (Xavier, 2020).

**Shimenawa Boundaries**

A thick straw rope, the shimenawa, often stretched between posts or circling trunks, stands out as an unmistakable border. The roughness of its twisted rice straw or hemp feels ancient and handmade, while crisp strips of white paper called shide flutter at intervals from its length. Together, rope and paper seem to amplify each other—the scratch against skin and the hush of moving air both catch the senses even before any words are read. The function is not to trap divinity inside or fence people out (Xavier, 2020; *Shinto Shrine Guide - Iconography, Objects, Superstitions in Japanese Shintoism*, 2010). Instead, shimenawa announces: "You are entering a place where your mindset should shift." In dense patches of foliage, the contrast between natural and crafted elements marks a zone where one slows, gazes upward, and breathes more quietly. Gaps left in the rope signal entry points—a prompt for the body to pause, relax shoulders, reset posture. With each annual replacement, the community gently reawakens the act of noticing boundaries, reminding everyone that sacred space only endures when it is continually cared for, not simply installed and forgotten (*Shinto Shrine Guide - Iconography, Objects, Superstitions in Japanese Shintoism*, 2010).

## Iwakura Stones

Some rocks, known as iwakura, command attention by their shape, size, or placement. Their natural forms—sometimes flat, sometimes upright, occasionally balanced so that sunlight hits them in a striking way—are left untouched by tools. A low shimenawa might mark the approach. Travelers find that footpaths curve around rather than over such stones. Offerings of salt, clear sake, or a leafy branch appear near the base on small dishes, never directly on top, showing respect by maintaining a bit of distance (Xavier, 2020). At the edge of a village or tucked beside old trees, iwakura carry the sense of being watched by something dignified, but not necessarily remote. Moss beds and crawling ferns encircle these rocks in green, softening steps and reducing noise, adding to the atmosphere of quiet observance. Where a large boulder sits alone, a traveler's own stance tends to echo the restraint shown by caretakers—shoulders square, gaze lowered, feet steady. Each gesture reinforces the lesson that honor lies in recognizing where not to tread as much as where to move.

### Wayfinding Torches

As dusk falls, pools of light appear along the winding approaches to shrines. Stone lanterns—tōrō—are solid and calm. Their surfaces bear the weathering of decades, sometimes centuries. At festival times, paper lanterns swing overhead, casting a warm, wavering glow. These lights do more than illuminate darkness; they set the rhythm of progress. Eyes track from lamp to lamp and feet slow as the path rises or bends. Crushed gravel underfoot crunches with every deliberate step. Edged paths, low hedges, or slightly raised borders mark the suggested walkways. There is no need for fences or ropes because the design itself teaches restraint. Stepped approaches, switchbacks, and planted verges create small pauses, inviting visitors to breathe in time with their stride. At intervals, a carefully placed pool or basin, a view through the trees, or a sudden clearing become new focal points. Light and path together create a choreography—one that shapes respectful movement by design (Xavier, 2020).

### Notice Boards

Near entrances and crossroads, wooden boards display simple illustrations of bowing, hand washing, or other gestures. These boards are generous and practical guides. Diagrams offer gentle instructions for newcomers who may never have visited a shrine before (*Shinto Shrine Guide - Iconography*,

*Objects, Superstitions in Japanese Shintoism*, 2010). Short stories explain why this precise spot matters. If a tree marks the resting place of a kami, or a stone signals gratitude for harvest rain, the text brings myth into daily understanding. Seasonal notices rotate through the year, linking practice to nature's cycles—cherry blossoms, summer heat, first snows. Instead of dictating rules, these signs extend invitations, saying: "Here is how you can join us in care and memory." Boards bridge the gap between the unfamiliar and the known, easing uncertainty without shaming curiosity. As readers move from marker to marker, lessons of etiquette become habits of attention, turning the whole site into a living script that is easy to follow and hard to forget.

Returning to the question at the chapter's start—when a rope circles an old cedar, does it protect the tree, or reshape our seeing?—these markers encourage careful presence, not just protection. Ropes, rocks, lanterns, and boards all invite us to tune our senses and learn a pace attuned to wonder. Through ordinary materials, the land becomes legible, and the path through it becomes an ongoing act of appreciation.

## Final Thoughts

Looking back on the places we've visited in this chapter, it becomes clear that mountains, rivers, and trees are much more than scenery in Japanese folk life. They shape what people do, how they move, and what they remember. When you walk by a river or step beneath an ancient cedar, there's a quiet invitation to listen and notice. Ropes, stones, lanterns, and small signs don't just protect nature—they help us see with fresher eyes. Each marker acts as a gentle reminder to slow down, be grateful, and take part in traditions that have connected communities for generations.

As you think about your own favorite places—the path you take to work, an old tree in a park, a bend in a local creek—consider how they quietly guide your actions without ever saying a word. In Japan, this idea of places shaping people is woven into daily life through countless gestures and stories. Paying attention to these living presences can deepen our sense of belonging and respect, not only for nature but also for each other. The world starts to feel more alive and connected when we let place, memory, and care flow together.

# Chapter 3: Ancestral Ties: Households, Memory, and Everyday Reverence

On a quiet weekday morning in Kyoto, the gentle habits of a household come quietly alive. A woman carefully pours a small cup of cool water, places a pinch of salt beside a solitary tangerine, and adjusts a delicate paper amulet above her kitchen doorway before heading out for the day. These simple actions, unhurried and humble, carry meanings deepened by history and care. As light filters through the room, dust softly dances in the air around a modest wooden shelf that holds these offerings, linking the everyday with something timeless. Later, when evening falls, her partner kneels before a wooden cabinet in the living room, lighting incense with a practiced hand, bowing once to honor a grandfather he never knew, and whispering words that echo gratitude and remembrance. Neither scene is marked by grandeur or ceremony, but both ground the household in a shared sense of respect, continuity, and belonging.

These quiet rituals—whether placing a fresh leaf on a tiny shrine or arranging names carefully inscribed on tablets—form a tapestry of reverence woven into daily life. They invite moments of pause amid routine, connecting present family members with ancestors and unseen guardians. This chapter invites you to step into the intimate spaces where these acts unfold: from the kamidana, a simple household shelf offering a place for spirits and gratitude, to the ancestral tablets and seasonal lanterns that brighten summer nights. Through exploring these everyday gestures, we glimpse how remembrance lives not just in grand festivals but in the steady rhythm of home, where memory, devotion, and place converge.

## Kamidana and Domestic Veneration

A simple wooden shelf, set high on the wall, holds a quiet presence in many Japanese homes. This is the kamidana – literally a "kami shelf" – an everyday space where families honor the unseen beings who watch over household life. Its location isn't chosen at random; placing it above eye level signals care and respect, inviting a gentle upward gaze each morning. The act of looking up, even briefly, nudges the mind into a space of gratitude and focus, as sunlight streaks across clean wood or dust motes drift in the early light. Dusting the shelf's edge with a damp cloth brings a faint aroma of forest, cool and crisp, and leaves behind a sense of readiness. In city apartments, the kamidana might hang just above a study desk or across from a window overlooking rooftops. In rural homes, it could settle near tatami mats and sliding doors that open to gardens. Even in small studios, someone living alone may find room for a slender ledge tucked in a quiet corner—its modest size never diminishing its meaning (Kamidana – David Chart's Blog, 2021).

Cleanliness and elevation become languages of reverence. By raising the kamidana out of daily bustle and keeping the area uncluttered, households mark this as a zone for attention. Such choices shape family rhythms, without words, reminding everyone to move a little more deliberately around the shelf: not tossing bags beneath it, not crowding it with everyday objects. When a person stands before the kamidana, the air feels a little fresher—set apart, simply by intention.

Offerings bring this space to life, asking for a moment of pause. Water glints in a tiny ceramic cup, cool and newly poured. A pinch of uncooked rice, white and plump, rests in a shallow vessel. Salt sparkles in another dish, crystalline and fine-grained. Each element comes from close at hand—the tap, the kitchen, the pantry—but carries wider meanings. Water refreshes and flows, echoing local springs and rivers. Rice recalls seasons of planting and harvest, drawing memory toward fields tended by hands now gone. Salt stands for cleansing, for new beginnings and safety. These gifts create a circle of giving: from home to kami, then back again, as most families eat the offerings after prayers are done. Sometimes sake is included, a slender glass bottle catching the midday light on the shelf, reminding all who pass that even familiar things can be tokens of thanks (Kamidana – David Chart's Blog, 2021).

Rhythms of care repeat through days and weeks. Many households change offerings with the turning of the sakaki leaves—a glossy evergreen branch often placed on either side of the shrine box—or whenever they tidy the shelf. The frequency shifts with work schedules, family needs, or simple forgetfulness. There's no single way; what matters is the gesture and the intent. For some, caring for the kamidana becomes a shared practice. Small children might help pour water, fingers steadying a cup, while elders arrange rice and check that the shelf remains bright and neat. The repetition weaves spiritual attention into daily routine, just as watering plants or wiping down a table does.

Some moments deepen these patterns. New Year brings a special renewal—the kamidana and all its objects are removed, carefully wiped, and returned with fresh o-fuda, which are sacred paper amulets received from a shrine. This annual act matches the energy of starting anew, mirroring spring cleaning in other cultures or the feeling of crisp sheets on a made bed. Parents may invite their children to join, showing how to bow together, how to place fragrant citrus or bright persimmons beside the cups. Not every family follows exactly the same script. Some adapt, shifting the day or skipping steps when routines get busy. What stays true is the wish for a good beginning, for luck and health to follow the new year (Kamidana – David Chart's Blog, 2021).

Connections reach beyond home walls. Offerings sometimes include seasonal produce: a smooth-skinned apple in autumn, a bundle of new onions in spring. These connect family practice to the cycles of local farms and markets, closing the gap between private ritual and regional landscape. Most kamidana hold at least one ofuda from a family's guardian shrine, linking household devotion to the larger web of shrines, priests, and festivals. Bringing home a fresh ofuda is a quiet act of belonging—the walk to a neighborhood shrine, the brief conversation with a priest, the return journey carrying a wrapped talisman nestled against other purchases. Setting the ofuda on the kamidana tucks community presence into daily life, making the invisible ties of place and ancestry a bit more tangible. As households maintain both kamidana and, often, ancestral altars (butsudan), these gestures plant seeds for deeper family remembrance—a theme that will unfold further in coming sections (Kamidana – David Chart's Blog, 2021).

## Butsudan and Ancestral Presence

The rhythms of daily life in many Japanese homes include quiet gestures of gratitude and reverence, anchored by two different altars: the kamidana, honoring protective kami, and the butsudan, centered around the family's ancestors. While the kamidana often rests high on a shelf, connecting the household to natural spirits outside, the butsudan usually sits at eye level or just above, inviting family members into moments of remembrance with those who came before. Both spaces hold water, flowers, and offerings, but the conversations woven through them diverge—one reaches out to place-spirits for protection, the other turns inward to the lineage that shaped the household (*Japan's Obon Festival: How Family Commemoration and Ancestral Worship Shapes Daily Life*, 2022).

## Memorial Tablets: Names anchor lineage in a visible form

Inside the butsudan, slender memorial tablets called ihai stand upright, often carved from lacquered wood. Each tablet carries the name of a departed ancestor, carefully brushed in black or gold calligraphy along with dates marking their lifespan. The arrangement may follow family lines—grandparents in one row, great-grandparents beyond. Sometimes a child's own given name echoes a character from these tablets, a silent thread connecting generations.

These tablets do not sit hidden away. In apartments, they may share the living room; in larger homes, they occupy a central alcove. As families gather nearby, the names catch a glance—sometimes sparking stories about the person behind each inscription. An elderly aunt might point to her mother's ihai and explain how her love of zinnias lives on in the flower choices for the altar. A parent may trace the kanji of a grandfather's name, helping a child recognize the same brushstroke in their own. Through these fleeting encounters, memory stays close, less like a formal ceremony and more like a gentle whisper reminding everyone where they come from. This visual map of lineage helps younger members find their place in the ongoing story, anchoring them in a sense of belonging.

## Ritual Simplicity: Incense and bows enact remembrance

There is no need for elaborate rituals to honor ancestors at the butsudan. The act begins with lighting incense—a scratch of a match, a slim stick tipped with glowing ember, smoke curling into still air. As the scent rises, family members fold their hands in gassho, pressing palms together, and bow their heads. Sometimes a single bow is enough, filled with intention and respect. Spoken words can be simple—a thank you for support, news about a child's first day of school, or a quiet hope for health.

No special training is required; children learn by watching adults, then imitate the movement with awkward fingers pressed tightly. The routine weaves remembrance into the ordinary flow of life. For some, the smell of incense triggers recollections of childhood mornings spent near the butsudan, while others associate it with the gentle presence of grandparents now gone. There's comfort in the accessibility of these acts—anyone can light a stick, offer a bow, say a few words. The barrier between generations softens as conversation becomes ongoing. Ancestors remain present not only on solemn days but folded into the fabric of daily routines (*Japan's Obon Festival: How Family Commemoration and Ancestral Worship Shapes Daily Life*, 2022).

Chapter 3: Ancestral Ties: Households, Memory, and Everyday Reverence

**Milestone Visits: Anniversaries and festivals renew bonds**

While everyday gestures keep memories alive, certain times of year draw families together around the butsudan for more focused remembrance. Death anniversaries, known as meinichi or nenki, bring relatives back to the ancestral home, sometimes from far across cities. On these appointed days, cleaning the butsudan becomes a shared project—children dust the wooden frame, teenagers arrange fresh flowers, adults prepare the favorite dishes of the departed. These meals carry memory into taste and smell: the sound of miso soup bubbling on the stove, the feel of sticky rice shaped by hand, the aroma of tea poured in silence.

Seasonal observances, like the spring and autumn equinoxes (Higan), serve as collective occasions for renewal. Families may pause their busy schedules to gather, acknowledge ancestors, and reflect together. These milestone visits build anticipation and give permission to slow down, offering structure to remembrance that daily life might otherwise scatter. Eating a relative's preferred sweet or telling a familiar story around the butsudan creates a sense of unity across ages and distances. The emotional warmth of these gatherings prepares the ground for community celebrations like Obon, when remembrance expands from individual households into a broader neighborhood and social network (*Japan's Obon Festival: How Family Commemoration and Ancestral Worship Shapes Daily Life*, 2022).

## Coexistence at Home: Shinto and Buddhist elements share space

Japanese homes often display both a kamidana and a butsudan, reflecting a layered heritage that holds space for both place-spirits and family lineage. The spatial choreography shapes the rhythm of the day: before meals, a quiet greeting to ancestors at the butsudan invites them to share in nourishment; before stepping outside, an acknowledgment at the kamidana seeks safe passage.

The kamidana typically sits higher, connecting to sky and nature, while the butsudan stands at a closer, approachable height. This arrangement doesn't require strict boundaries—some homes incorporate seasonal flowers or art objects in the same room as the altars, blending daily aesthetics with ritual care. The presence of both altars supports an inclusive atmosphere, welcoming spirits of place and kin alike. Through this coexistence, families nurture gratitude for both the natural world and for the people whose stories shape their own (*Japan's Obon Festival: How Family Commemoration and Ancestral Worship Shapes Daily Life*, 2022).

## Obon as Homecoming of the Departed

While household altars anchor remembrance year-round, Obon transforms entire communities into spaces of welcome.

## Chapter 3. Ancestral Ties: Households, Memory, and Everyday Reverence

The quiet gestures at a butsudan—the lighting of incense, simple bows before the family tablets—set a gentle rhythm that prepares households for another kind of gathering. When summer arrives, this personal practice grows outward, reaching into the neighborhood streets and temple courtyards as families ready themselves for reunion with those who once walked beside them. Children help their parents clean entryways and set up lanterns, eager and solemn at the same time. Conversations drift from what to cook for dinner to which cousin will arrive first, blending daily routine and seasonal anticipation.

Guiding Fires: Lanterns symbolize pathways for returning souls. At dusk, neighbors emerge onto porches, each holding their own paper or glass-covered lantern. The flicker of candlelight joins a hundred others on street corners and temple paths. As flames steady in the warm air, adults quietly recall faces long gone, while children marvel at the glow. Some families cluster around a single lantern, placing offerings—a tangerine, cup of tea, small rice cake—by its side so ancestors may find their way home. This gentle illumination is both practical and symbolic: it makes the invitation visible, acknowledging absence without erasing memory. Lanterns are hung not only at doorways but sometimes floated downstream in ceremonies called toro-nagashi, their drifting lights carrying hopes and gratitude into the shadows (Agoda Travel Guides, 2025). Lighting a candle for the departed is a gesture found across cultures, but the gathered hush of Obon has its own warmth—a collective pause that honors presence and return.

Dance of Belonging: Bon odori unites generations through steps and songs. Each neighborhood hosts its own circle dance, drawing people of all ages to the open spaces beneath strings of lanterns. Steps are simple, often repeated in easy patterns. A toddler can follow along beside a grandparent, newcomers are gently folded into the group, and laughter mixes with the beat of taiko drums. The central yagura, a platform for musicians and leaders, anchors the circle and becomes a beacon that draws dancers closer. Songs change from region to region; some lyrics remember local heroes, others tell of harvests or mountains nearby. In joining the circle, everyone becomes part of a living archive, preserving stories through motion and refrain. Moving together under moonlit skies, the festival crowd blurs lines of age and role, transforming a park or temple courtyard into a temporary home for shared memory (Agoda Travel Guides, 2025). These community dances echo ideas explored elsewhere in this book: place-based rhythms, regional variation, and the way festivals shape collective identity across Japan's agricultural calendar.

Graveside Care: Cleaning and offerings renew obligations. During Obon, families travel—sometimes across prefectures—to ancestral graves. It's common to see children piling into cars with bags of fresh flowers, rags and buckets rattling in the trunk alongside favorite foods of the deceased. At the cemetery, the visit unfolds as gentle work: moss gets scrubbed away, stones washed and dried, old water replaced. Flowers are arranged, incense lit, and sometimes oranges or sweets are set down on the cool stone. Relatives might kneel together to clear stray leaves or share memories of the person whose name is carved before them. For children, these trips become lessons: where the family came from, how to trace roots backward, why these annual efforts matter. What seems an act of duty reveals itself as care—life reaffirmed by tending what endures (Agoda Travel Guides, 2025).

Farewell Rituals: Sending-off gestures close the sacred visit. When Obon winds down, lanterns are taken from their hooks and candles allowed to gutter out. Families gather for a final meal, perhaps savoring leftover somen noodles or manju, before one last pinch of incense curls skyward from the altar. Some regions send floating lanterns down rivers to guide spirits back, while others offer a last cup of water at a doorway, a sign of thanks for protection and guidance. Children learn to bow deeply, expressing gratitude and letting go. These farewells mark the transition from sacred time back into the everyday, helping every generation carry forward the presence of those who are gone but never lost (Agoda Travel Guides, 2025).

As the festival's rituals ripple through neighborhoods—from lantern-lit streets to graveled temple yards—they spark renewed conversations about family lineage, shared stories, and the responsibilities tied to inherited names. Obon reminds everyone why remembrance matters, shaping the ethics that surface each time a name is written, a story retold, or a promise kept to ancestors. Soon, this thread leads directly into the next chapter's exploration of how names, records, and ethical conduct carry ancestral legacies into the future.

## Names, Lineage, and Ethical Memory

Obon's lanterns and dances bring ancestors home in a blaze of light once a year. Names and everyday habits, though, keep that connection alive through the quiet rhythms of daily life. In Japanese households, naming a child is never just about choosing pleasant sounds. Often, families select kanji characters for children's names that pick up qualities or memories from admired forebears. For example, parents might sit with grandparents recalling a late relative who embodied perseverance. They may choose a character like " " (nin, meaning endurance) or " " (kō, meaning steady). Sometimes, elders share stories around the table—how Aunt Sachiko rebuilt after hardship or how Great-grandfather was trusted for his honest words. These stories turn naming into a gentle lesson: each new name is both a hope for the future and a thread tying the present to the family's living story. Even when parents honor tradition, they can vary pronunciation or combine fresh characters, finding a balance between remembrance and personal identity. In this way, every name becomes a gesture of respect and a wish for the child's unfolding strengths (Kumar, 2023).

Family records stand as silent witnesses to these choices and connections, offering more than a technical list of births, deaths, and marriages. Many homes keep household genealogies, temple registries, or memorial scrolls tucked

## Chapter 3: Ancestral Ties: Households, Memory, and Everyday Reverence

away in drawers or displayed near ancestral altars. These documents often carry brief descriptions beside each name—"cared for sick neighbors," "replanted the cherry tree after the storm"—transforming facts into stories. During a family gathering, children might hear an elder explain how an ancestor's kindness passed down as a family value, making history feel close and tender. In recent years, some families scan old photos or digitize handwritten ledgers so that younger relatives overseas can see their heritage without risking damage to precious originals. Old and new methods blend, letting distant cousins visit virtual archives while older hands still brush dust from paper pages. These practices offer models for anyone seeking to preserve their own family memory—combining story and record-keeping in ways that foster feeling as well as fact (Kumar, 2023).

Inheritance carries more than objects; it transmits virtues. Everyday actions are seen as reflections on one's lineage. A diligent student, careful at school, is honoring ancestors whose sacrifices made education possible. When siblings sweep the porch together before guests arrive, the act echoes generations of shared care. Parents sometimes turn small moments—helping a neighbor carry groceries, keeping a promise at work—into reminders that one's conduct shapes not just personal reputation but the dignity of all who came before and those yet to come. Community service or teaching a skill may be explained as gratitude paid forward, an answer to support once received from kin or mentors. In this cultural framework, ethical memory is not abstract; it weaves through every choice, giving purpose and belonging to daily routine (Kumar, 2023).

Memory also means facing mistakes with honesty. Apologies within families are valued for strengthening trust, not exposing weakness. When someone returns a forgotten debt or repairs a careless remark, the action repairs not only relationships in the present, but also honors the family's ongoing story. Parents may recount times when older relatives made amends, sharing how lessons learned prevented future harm. The courage to admit wrongdoing becomes part of what gets handed down—a message that repair matters more than perfection, and that taking responsibility helps the whole family move forward together (Kumar, 2023).

Across each of these strands—names rich with intention, storied records gently tended, ethics lived quietly each day, and acts of honest repair—a tapestry emerges. Kamidana's daily offerings mark the presence of spirit in ordinary routines; butsudan's quiet glow holds remembrance in the home; Obon gathers everyone for communal joy and loss. Ethical memory joins them, turning reverence into something active and nurturing. Through these customs, ancestors become guides not just for festival days but for every moment where care, patience, or humility matter. This lived tapestry opens a space for reflection: the past moves with us, shaping today's choices, and reaching gently into tomorrow (Kumar, 2023).

## Bringing It All Together

Throughout these pages, we've followed the gentle flow of daily rituals that keep households connected—to their own sense of gratitude, to ancestors, and to the living world outside. Each gesture—offering a pinch of salt, lighting incense, straightening an amulet—anchors people in something bigger than routine. These aren't grand performances but quiet acts that add meaning to breakfast tables and doorways alike. Simple as they may seem, household practices like tending the kamidana or gathering at the butsudan help shape a feeling of belonging, passing on stories even when words are few.

As we move through mornings, seasons, and family gatherings, these small rituals encourage us to pause, reflect, and remember. By keeping ancestral names close and sharing in yearly festivals like Obon, families weave together tradition, memory, and hope for the future. Every shelf, tablet, lantern, and cup connects one day to the next, inviting anyone—no matter their background—to experience continuity and care. Looking back, it becomes clear: the heart of these customs isn't just about reverence—it's about living with presence, respect, and gratitude, every single day.

# Chapter 4: Seasons of Meaning: Calendars, Rites, and Agricultural Rhythms

Imagine the city of Tokyo as midnight approaches, where skyscrapers blaze with neon lights counting down the final seconds of the year. Here, the new year flicks on like a switch--a sharp moment marked by digital clocks and fresh resolutions saved in smartphone apps. Now, shift your gaze to a quiet seaside town in Shikoku. The scene changes completely: ordinary doorways transform with pine boughs, bamboo shoots, and twisted straw ropes, turning thresholds into sacred gates. Families gather in hushed anticipation, waiting as the gentle tolling of shrine bells rolls across the night sky to announce the start of the year. These two moments—one brisk and modern, the other slow and ritual-laden—show how time itself can be felt and celebrated in very different ways.

By looking closely at these contrasting rhythms—the clock-driven managerial year versus the cyclical agricultural-spiritual year—we begin to see how Japanese folklore weaves deep meaning into each day and season. This chapter invites you to step through that symbolic doorway, exploring how rituals at home, in the fields, and along village streets shape communal life. From New Year's decorations that mark renewal, to rice planting prayers and lively neighborhood festivals, the patterns of renewal and boundary-crossing give form to the calendar, grounding abstract time in shared human experience.

## New Year Thresholds and Renewals

Sliding open the front door, you are greeted by a crisp hush that hangs in the New Year's air. The entryway is alive with decorations: a pine-and-bamboo arrangement standing tall beside the threshold, rice straw ropes twisted and adorned with paper strips above the entrance, and somewhere nearby, the faint smell of dried citrus mingling with fresh wood. There's a sense of pause, as if every object has been quietly arranged to mark this space—and this time—as something special. Japanese homes and neighborhoods at New Year become stages for ritual renewal, their entrances transformed into welcome mats for good fortune and clean beginnings. These customs give shape to the turning of the calendar, resetting not just clocks but feelings of possibility.

As we saw with family altars and daily gestures, the turn of the year offers a larger canvas for the same impulse: renewing bonds, inviting blessings, and setting the tone for what follows. New Year thresholds do more than decorate; they announce the desire to start again well, with both household and spirit ready for what lies ahead.

## Purifying Entrances: Inviting Fortune, Marking Boundaries

At almost every front door, you'll discover shimekazari—twisted rice straw festooned with sprigs of fern, bitter orange, and zigzag paper strips called shide. Some are ornate; others, simple enough for children to help make. Along paths or large gates, kadomatsu appear with their upright pine boughs and bamboo stalks cut at sharp angles. Both signal a warm invitation to Toshigami-sama, the seasonal deity said to bring blessings for health, prosperity, and growth into each home. At the same time, these decorations serve as shields, warding off unlucky spirits and reminding residents to move through this border with care and gratitude (*Decoding the Traditional Japanese New Year Decorations*, 2024).

The act of putting up these decorations is often a family effort, done together in late December after a thorough cleaning—osoji—to clear out last year's dust and energy. The cycle of placement and removal forms its own kind of rhythm. In mid-January, families take down shimekazari and kadomatsu, sometimes burning them in Dondoyaki bonfires at shrines or temples. Watching flames carry away last year's troubles while prayers rise on the smoke is a scene repeated across neighborhoods, binding the sacred and everyday together. Even those simply passing by feel the atmosphere of quiet mindfulness these customs create.

# Chapter 4. Seasons of Meaning: Calendars, Rites, and Agricultural Rhythms

## First Shrine Visit: Hatsumode and Shared Hopes

In the early hours of January 1st, lantern-lit shrines fill with bundled families and streams of visitors. People warm their hands against the winter air, clutching coins and little envelopes for offerings. The mood is at once festive and serious. Children laugh, elders bow in silence, friends stand shoulder-to-shoulder waiting to pray. Many people drop a coin, bow twice, clap twice, and offer a silent wish for the coming year. Small slips of paper called omikuji reveal fortunes—some hopeful, some less so—and wooden ema plaques quickly fill with handwritten hopes or thanks, hung together for the gods to read. These rituals turn private anxieties or dreams into actions witnessed and shared, weaving personal intentions into the broader tapestry of community life (*Decoding the Traditional Japanese New Year Decorations*, 2024).

Starting the year with intentional choices—prayer, reflection, even laughter—connects the smallest household routine to a countrywide pulse. As you'll see in later chapters, this network of prayer and offering echoes how individual and communal rituals intertwine, creating strong lines of belonging from one person, through family, outward to neighborhood and nation.

## Auspicious Firsts: Sunrise, Dreams, and Calligraphy

While calendars count midnight as the beginning, for many, the New Year truly starts with hatsuhinode—the first sunrise.

People climb hillsides or beaches, eyes fixed east, waiting for the day's first gold rim to crest over the landscape. This simple act draws attention to nature's time, folding human hopes into the movement of sun and season. Afterward comes talk of hatsuyume, the 'first dream' one remembers after lying down on New Year's night. Stories say certain images—a hawk, Mt. Fuji, an eggplant—foretell luck, turning sleep itself into a source of meaning. In some homes, children and parents gather for kakizome, the first calligraphy of the year. Brushes dip into ink, and words like hope, spring, or harmony flow onto white sheets, their strokes releasing intention into the world. These traditions offer ways to catch wishes in tangible acts, shaping the mind and heart for days to come (*Decoding the Traditional Japanese New Year Decorations*, 2024).

### Gift Cycles: Networks of Reciprocity and Care

A gentle knock signals a delivery—on New Year's morning, mail carriers arrive with thick bundles of nengajo postcards. Each card marks a line in the web of connection: friend to friend, coworker to supervisor, neighbor to neighbor. Messages are brief, decorated with zodiac animals, sometimes carrying inside jokes or photos from the past year. Children look forward to otoshidama, small envelopes holding crisp bills presented with quiet ceremony by older relatives. The careful giving and receiving of oseibo—year-end gifts exchanged among colleagues, clients, or landlords—reminds everyone that stewardship and thanks cross generational and social boundaries.

Chapter 4: Seasons of Meaning: Calendars, Rites, and Agricultural Rhythms

These gift cycles echo the layered networks and obligations found throughout Japanese ritual, as described in Chapters 3 and 6. The shape of each exchange—postcard, envelope, box of fruit—embodies both blessing and duty. One child, wide-eyed, opens a red-and-white envelope and feels recognized, while an office worker pens greetings, thinking not only of courtesy but also of the chance for a warmer relationship next year. Through these actions, the circle of renewal ripples outward, blending personal memory with shared custom.

Once the home's thresholds are marked and the first prayers offered, attention turns outward to the fields—another site of renewal where the rhythms of rice and rain set the pace for community life. Just as doors are purified at New Year, so too are landscapes prepared for the planting, gratitude, and labor that bind village and town together.

## Planting, Harvest, and Rice Rites

Moving from the household's purified threshold to the open sky of the fields, villagers gather in early spring as a fresh wind stirs and sunlight glimmers on cold water. Bells sound at the edge of muddy paddies, and a Shinto priest steps forward in white robes—his feet steady and slow, his breath visible in the morning air. Norito prayers begin, their words flowing like water: they do not command the earth or the weather but ask, humbly, for blessing and protection. Salt, sake, and cleaned rice grains are cupped in careful hands and set gently before small wooden stands at the field's edge. These offerings feel less like payment and more like an invitation—a quiet reminder that each season's outcome depends on partnership with land, rivers, and the unseen spirits known as kami (*Shinto*, n.d.). Farmers kneel in rows; nearby, shopkeepers and children shuffle for a better view. All stand together as the prayer ends—community as equal participants, not just observers.

At planting, the field becomes a stage. The first planters often wear loose white garments, a sign of harae or purity, echoing beliefs that humans can return themselves to wholeness through deliberate action and ritual renewal (*Shinto*, n.d.). Movements slow down: hands dip seedling roots into thick mud, people sing rhythmically, taiko drums thump like heartbeat underfoot. No one rushes. Each gesture, from the dipping of rice stalks to the patting of soil, gathers intention—care flows into every handful of dirt. There is pride in using last year's plumpest grains as new seed. For older farmers, this choice tastes like memory; for children, it feels like hope, building a link across generations. At some schools, classes take half a day off in May to come watch and help. Laughter drifts, boots splash, and teachers explain the old names for tools and songs. This moment frames rice not just as food but as inheritance and connection.

As the green shoots ripen to gold, families sense the change in the air before anyone says a word. When the harvest comes, gratitude takes center stage. Before eating the new rice at home, many bring polished grains to the shrine. The first bowl belongs to the kami. This pause marks respect—it reminds everyone that enjoying the harvest follows only after a

## Chapter 4: Seasons of Meaning: Calendars, Rites, and Agricultural Rhythms

wordless nod to all that made it possible (*Shinto*, n.d.). In the imperial palace, a ceremony called Niinamesai carries these same themes, but villagers gather too, setting aside normal business to share the work and the reward. Neighbors may trade small packets of new rice, or school lunches might feature the year's first harvest, turning an ordinary meal into something quietly special. Sharing isn't just symbolic; dividing the season's first gifts spreads luck and well-being, almost as though every bowl of cooked rice still holds a taste of sunlight and prayer.

With the fields cleared, celebration moves indoors or to broad mats outside. Plates pile high with sticky rice balls, local herbs, grilled river fish, and delicate sweets shaped like autumn leaves. Elders reminisce about years when floods changed everything or when a late warm spell brought unusual sweetness to the rice. Younger relatives lean close, listening for familiar jokes and stories about clever foxes or unlucky harvests. Kagura dances fill the space between bites—dancers depict gods teasing mortals, or animals coaxing rain from jealous clouds. Some gestures are big and playful; others, simple hand movements tied to centuries-old myths. Songs spill from tired throats, blending thanks with longing and humor. Food doesn't just fill hunger; it anchors memories of place and people, teaching each generation how much the land gives—and how much care and attention it needs in return. Recipes handed down in worn notebooks or whispered beside smoky stoves keep alive both flavor and belonging.

All these field-based ceremonies shape the community's rhythm, blending practical work with a spirit of cooperation and reverence. Purity rituals, avoidance of impurity, and collective care echo far beyond planting and harvest, showing up later in household cleaning days, neighborhood festivals, and quiet moments of personal gratitude. This rhythm of planting and thanks prepares communities for the next thresholds—times when old misfortune is cast out and new balance is invited in. The story moves from sturdy order in muddy fields to the flexible, spirited hinges of the seasons that follow, like Setsubun or the equinoxes—moments when the calendar itself seems to tip and reset (*Shinto*, n.d.).

## Transitions of Spring and Autumn

Where rice rites aligned communities with field cycles, seasonal boundaries call households to mark threshold moments with care and intention. The Japanese calendar pivots around these liminal times, with Setsubun signaling the cold's end in early February and Higan equinoxes balancing light and dark halfway through spring and autumn. These days invite families to turn inward for protection, cleansing, and gentle realignment before joining neighborhood celebrations.

**Bean Scattering: Clearing Out Demons and Inviting Fortune**

On the evening of Setsubun, homes fill with quick motion and laughter as mamemaki—the bean-scattering ritual—begins. Small hands scoop roasted soybeans, the fukumame or "lucky beans," and scatter them through doorways, window ledges, or even across tatami mats. Each throw is punctuated by the chant "Oni wa soto! Fuku wa uchi!" sending ogres out and beckoning good fortune inside. This practice transforms an invisible season shift into sound, movement, and shared intent. After scattering, family members crouch or kneel to collect and eat a number of beans matching their age, plus one more, bringing protective energy inside their bodies. Sometimes unshelled peanuts take the place of soybeans, making cleanup easier while keeping the symbolism intact (*Setsubun*, 2016). Supermarkets brim with bags of beans and paper oni masks weeks ahead, turning city streets into playful stages. Alongside beans, some regions hang dried sardine heads on holly sprigs by the door, a pungent signal to any unseen spirit that this household stands protected (Team, 2022). More recently, the tradition of eating a whole eho-maki sushi roll in silence, facing the lucky direction for the year, has gained popularity. Each uncut cylinder eaten without pause becomes a tiny act of alignment, a full-body wish carried into the months ahead (*Setsubun*, 2016).

**Mask Play: Transforming Fear into Ritual Theater**

Paper oni masks bring make-believe into living rooms and shrines, blurring lines between play, scare, and education. Usually, a family member—often the head of the house or someone born under that year's zodiac sign—slips on the fierce, red-faced demon mask and stomps through the home's corridors. Children squeal and aim handfuls of beans at the intruding "oni," practicing how to face anxiety and uncertainty in a space where guardianship and humor soften the lesson (*Setsubun*, 2016). At temples, monks don elaborate costumes and stage dramatic chases, their booming steps echoing moral tales about courage and inner strength. Blessings and chants flow alongside beans, reinforcing that difficulty is not banished alone but recast into story, song, and safe confrontation. Through this annual theater, adults and children rehearse emotional balance together.

**Boundary Cleaning: Resetting the Household Edge**

As spring or autumn turns, cleaning takes center stage. Doorways are swept free of leaves and dust, genkan entryways aired out, futon and cushions hung to capture fresh sunlight. Shoji screens slide open to welcome in shifting breezes and slanting sunbeams, marking subtle changes in the world outside. Beyond simple tidying, these gestures recalibrate the threshold between ordinary space and sacred shelter. Higan, observed at both vernal and autumnal equinoxes, draws attention to ancestral ties as families visit graves, weed plots, and set fresh flowers and incense. In caring for ancestor sites, households extend their sense of boundary beyond the immediate home, weaving care for the dead into the daily project of balance. Children may help sweep gravestones or light candles, learning that spiritual health grows from small acts of tending, just as much as from grand ceremony (Team, 2022).

## Seasonal Foods: Tasting the Turning Year

Seasonal food bridges the external calendar with the body's own rhythm. During the seven-day Higan periods, kitchens simmer nanakusa-gayu, a gentle porridge made from seven spring herbs, which soothes the stomach after winter's heavier fare. In autumn, sticky chestnut rice and savory mushrooms arrive on plates, joined by bright yellow chrysanthemum petals floating in tea or pressed into sweets. Botamochi and ohagi, sweet rice cakes coated in bean paste, appear at both equinoxes, their round shapes and grainy textures promising protection and unity. Eating these foods is physical attunement—a soft reset that aligns taste, warmth, and even color with the changing air. Menu shifts nudge families into a new pace, whether resting limbs with warming stews or embracing longer light with refreshing side dishes (*Setsubun*, 2016).

Having reset their doorways and bodies, families step into streets where shared routes carry neighborhood memory forward into public celebration. These private recalibrations prepare households to join the swelling energy of local matsuri, linking individual seasonal transitions with the joy and memory of collective festival life.

## Local Matsuri as Social Memory

Having tuned personal and household rhythms to the season's turning—sweeping thresholds, cooking with early greens—we now step into the streets where entire neighborhoods enact their shared calendar. Festivals, or matsuri, transform districts into moving sanctuaries of memory. Here, spiritual meaning moves from private routines to collective gestures that fill public spaces with layered sounds, scents, and colors. These gatherings do more than mark seasonal change; they map lived experience onto the city itself, making each street corner and crossroads part of a living archive (*Tokyo Local Culture Guide: Traditions & Modern Customs*, 2025).

### Portable Shrines: Mikoshi parades spread blessings through streets

Mikoshi processions bring the heart of the shrine out among the people. Groups of neighbors gather to lift the heavy portable shrine together, hoisting it on thick wooden beams, shoulders pressed close, hands gripping polished rails still sticky with summer humidity. The whole structure glides, rocks, and bounces in rhythm with coordinated chants—a purposeful stirring that invites the kami's attention. At key intersections, teams surge forward or sway side-to-side, splashing cool water over feet and pavement, an echo of purification rites. Each route is not random but follows streets mapped by generations before—always pausing at a neighborhood bridge, always stopping near an old corner well. These brief halts reactivate nodes of local significance, restoring sacred attention to places easily overlooked during the city's hurried days. The clatter of coins in donation boxes, flashes of silk sashes, and the syncopated shouts draw all ages into the choreography, making the event feel less like performance and more like vital, recurring practice (*Tokyo Local Culture Guide: Traditions & Modern Customs*, 2025).

**Craft Revival: Floats showcase artisanal lineages**

Festival floats, or dashi, roll slowly along narrow streets, gleaming in sunlight and lantern glow. Their panels carry the marks of countless hands—wooden carvings shaped by chisels handed down, brocade banners stitched with dyed threads, lacquer that gives off its own faint sweetness. As children help secure ropes or polish brass bells, elders tell stories about joiners who fit frames without nails and weavers whose hems survive decades of rain and festival use. Guilds, merchant houses, and artisan families sponsor these floats, entwining their work with the yearly rites. Apprenticeship happens in real time: a teenager learns the precise wrist motion needed to tie an anchor knot, following her uncle's hand exactly as his grandfather showed him. The pride of seeing one's handiwork displayed in the parade underlines how festivals keep both income and reputation circulating within the district. Every touch—the rough rope, the smooth lacquered wood, the clang of tools during last-minute repairs—turns festival preparation into a workshop of embodied memory (*Tokyo Local Culture Guide: Traditions & Modern Customs*, 2025).

### Song Repertoires: Chants preserve dialect and lore

Rhythm and voice bind festival participants across generations. In the hours leading up to dusk, clusters of drummers and flutists rehearse hayashi—chant-and-drum patterns unique to each area. Lyrics spill out in regional dialect, rolling vowels or clipped consonants that may sound unfamiliar even to fellow Tokyoites. Lines memorialize storms survived, bridges rebuilt, remarkable healers, or legendary distant traders. Here, language acts not just as communication but as a vessel for place-based history. Children walk in step with adults, learning when to clap, which lines demand a strong shout, which phrases soften into lullaby. Melodies shift gently over time, but core syllables and sequences anchor communal memory, ensuring history lives not only in documents but also in voices raised together, breath after breath (*Tokyo Local Culture Guide: Traditions & Modern Customs*, 2025).

### Route Significance: Paths trace ancient borders and bonds

The shape of each matsuri unfolds through the procession's chosen path. Old maps reveal that routes often trace irrigation channels, skirt vanished boundary stones, or connect sets of shrines that once protected the city's edge. Stopping points serve as reminders: past disaster sites invite offerings for safe seasons ahead, while market corners recall alliances between neighboring craftspeople. Each time the mikoshi pauses beside a capped well or beneath a faded stone torii, neighbors retell why this corner matters. You can read a festival's meaning directly from the land by watching where the group slows, noting spots decorated with cut paper or special lanterns, listening for bits of family story woven into the celebrant's instructions. These annual rounds refresh unwritten contracts between residents, sustaining trust and identity that may never appear in city records but persist in steps, voices, and shared effort (Tokyo Local Culture Guide: Traditions & Modern Customs*, 2025).

Festival movement leaves an impression that lasts after the lanterns have dimmed and drums grown silent. For those who follow along, each mikoshi bearing, song verse, and float turn offers a way to tune your own sense of time and belonging. Watching a procession reminds you that spiritual practice can be as much about walking your neighborhood, listening, and joining in small tasks as about formal prayer. The weeks spent preparing, repairing, remembering, and performing become their own kind of archive—one that you carry home, ready to surface again as the next season approaches. Soon, stories carved in wood and sung in chorus will lead us deeper into folklore and the power of material symbols carried forward in every festival year.

## Final Thoughts

As we've explored, New Year in Japan isn't just a matter of switching the calendar or counting down under neon lights. It's an experience packed with feeling, tradition, and a sense that time itself can be shaped by our actions—whether through cleaning a doorway, hanging pine branches, sharing postcards, or waiting for the sunrise. Simple objects and familiar routines carry a bigger meaning when they're part of this shared ritual, turning homes, streets, and even meals into places where the past and future brush up against each other for a moment. As one year turns into another, these customs invite everyone to look forward with hope and appreciation, while staying anchored in community and memory.

Watching the rhythm of city and countryside, resolution and ritual, we see how Japanese folklore gives shape to days and seasons. The threshold at New Year becomes both a real place and a symbol—a spot where possibility opens up and daily habits are charged with intention. In different corners of the country, people find comfort and motivation not just in marking time, but in making meaning together. This approach to beginnings lingers through the weeks that follow, guiding hearts and hands as we all step into what comes next.

# Chapter 5: Tales with Teeth and Tails: Folklore as Cultural Code

It's easy to think of the animal spirits in Japanese stories as just charming characters or scary creatures added for fun. But these foxes, raccoon dogs, and mountain spirits aren't simply decorations; they carry messages that go far beyond their playful or eerie appearances. Foxes testing promises, tanuki poking fun at pride, and mountain voices encouraging patience all act like a kind of language. They teach us about welcoming guests properly, sharing what we have, and how people and nature can understand each other. When you look at these stories closely, these creatures reveal lessons about honesty, kindness, and balance instead of just being magical beings.

Starting with the clever fox, whose shape-shifting is more than trickery, this chapter explores how these stories work as guides for everyday life. The fox's disguises reflect our own challenges with truth and trust, while the raccoon dog brings lightness and humor that soften life's difficulties. Mountain spirits offer wisdom about endurance and community care. Together, they show us how folklore serves as a cultural code, helping us see familiar tales in new ways and live with greater respect and connection to the world around us.

# Kitsune and Fox Wisdom

Fox tales in Japanese folklore run much deeper than clever distractions or playful tricks. They work as layered codes: a single story entertains, warns, and sparkles with sly humor all at once, but also carries the values that shape a household, a village, even a season's harvest. To truly read them, you must pay close attention to context—who is telling the story, at what time of year, and which needs sit just beneath the surface. In homes where rice offerings are made to fox spirits at New Year or autumn festivals, the stories echo real-world practices and seasonal concerns introduced earlier in this book. The lessons hidden in fox wisdom blend seamlessly with the rhythms of place and ritual (Jason, 2025).

**Shapeshifting Ethics**

Transformation sits at the heart of most kitsune stories. When a fox takes human shape or mimics a merchant, it creates uncertainty, but the purpose isn't just spectacle—it's a test. Leaders in a town might meet a traveling salesman offering miracle wares. Later, they discover he was a fox in disguise, exposing their own greed or vanity. Everyone listening learns to trust not simply in what someone appears to be, but in how they act under pressure. These tales reward kindness and make listeners question their first judgments. By showing that anyone can shift form, fox tales teach humility and adaptability. Certainty becomes a trap; curiosity and gentle caution become survival skills (Jason, 2025). Listeners soon realize these narratives aren't only about magical creatures— they're guides for surviving a world full of change.

**Inari Connections**

The presence of foxes on shrine markers, offertory stands, and stone gates links stories of kitsune directly to agricultural life. Many small shrines across Japan, whether set by rice fields or tucked into urban neighborhoods, hold statues of white foxes —the servants and messengers of Inari, kami of rice and prosperity. People leave grain, sake, or fried tofu at these spots, asking for good harvests or business success. In tale after tale, the fox responds to generosity with abundance: crops ripen, misfortune lifts. But the pattern also runs both ways. If someone steals from a neighbor or takes more than their share at the shrine, the next harvest may fail. Wastefulness brings trouble. In this way, the stories frame prosperity as a shared outcome, earned through honest effort, gratitude, and careful stewardship. The fox does not simply grant wealth; it upholds a contract rooted in labor and respect for the land. These same images and motifs will reappear in the next chapter when readers encounter foxes carved onto torii gates and votive tablets, reinforcing the visual-narrative loop between folk story and sacred space (Jason, 2025). Regional differences abound as well, with each place adding its own layer—sea foxes in island villages or competitions at harvest festivals—yet every version keeps this lesson alive.

**Marriage Motifs**

Another thread running through fox tales centers on marriage—not just as romance, but as an agreement shaped by secrecy, trust, and mutual care. A familiar plot begins with a man meeting a mysterious woman and marrying her, often after rescuing or helping a fox. He enjoys happiness until pushed by others or his own curiosity to break a promise: never to peek at her true form or ask where she goes. Once the secret is uncovered, the fox-wife vanishes, sometimes leaving behind children or gifts, but taking the sense of magic and balance with her. These stories pose hard questions: Is honesty always the highest good, or does respecting boundaries show greater love? When you encounter a fox-bride tale, listen for clues about loyalty, discretion, and the everyday risks of living closely with others. These plots mirror worries in real communities—how easy it is for trust to shatter, and how hard true intimacy can be to maintain (Jason, 2025). The listener is left wondering if knowing everything is less valuable than holding some things sacred.

**Trickster Pedagogy**

Fox stories rarely punish with force. Instead, pranks target those who overreach—an official who taxes too harshly, a merchant who cheats, a villager grown proud. Through illusions or playful swaps, the powerful fall from their pedestals, learning to laugh at themselves or return ill-gotten gains. In one example, a greedy tax collector wakes to find his riches turned to leaves, the villagers giggling nearby. Embarrassment, not revenge, puts things right. Justice becomes an act of putting the world back in balance, with laughter acting as both salve and lesson. These endings encourage flexibility—no one remains stuck in shame, and even tricked figures can find their way back into the fold. While kitsune tales cut with precision, teaching wit and self-awareness, the pages ahead promise tanuki stories where communal joy and belly-laughs soften the edges of moral learning (Jason, 2025).

## Tanuki, Humor, and Generosity

After the sly illusions of the kitsune, the world of tanuki stories opens with a different mood. Both creatures hold power to transform, yet the raccoon dog works its magic not by outsmarting individuals but by enveloping whole communities in laughter. The tanuki's playful tricks and love for plenty soften tensions, turning everyday moments into gentle reminders that life can be faced with warmth and humor. Where foxes revealed flaws, tanuki encouraged villagers to laugh at themselves, building bridges through shared amusement rather than sharp tests of character (Ajayi, 2024).

**Playful Illusions & Tavern Imagery**

Tanuki stories burst with scenes where silly pranks teach lessons without bruised egos. A classic moment unfolds when a greedy merchant thinks he's struck gold—only for his heavy coins to turn into dry leaves as soon as the tanuki trots away. Faces drop, tempers flare, but the sting never lingers. Instead, embarrassment gives way to sheepish smiles or shared jokes. Officials and merchants alike become the butt of comic justice, their pride gently punctured in front of giggling witnesses. Instead of exposing vice with shame or pain, these tales offer a friendly nudge: greed, pomp, and self-importance look foolish under the spotlight of a clever joke (Ajayi, 2024).

The tanuki's mischief rarely leads to lasting harm. Trickery becomes a soft-edged tool, allowing communities to vent grievances with powerful people in safe, indirect ways. Jabs at authority slip in like a well-timed punchline, never outright defiance but always a call for fairness and moderation. This atmosphere turns folklore gatherings into workshops for community repair, where flaws are teased out, laughed over, and mended with grins instead of punishments. Humor does what heated argument cannot; it cools tempers and resets perspective so people leave lighter, more ready to forgive and share responsibility.

## Chapter 5: Tales with Teeth and Tails: Folklore as Cultural Code

Stepping from street corners into lamplit taverns, the tone lightens even more. Stories tell of tanuki pounding their round bellies like drums, setting a rhythm that draws villagers in. Warm sake flows, plates pile high with food, and strangers find themselves welcomed as old friends beneath paper lanterns. The air thrums with laughter as the tanuki's generosity grows almost magical: cups refill by themselves, songs fill the rafters, and no one is left outside or hungry. These exaggerated feasts were more than escapist fantasy—they gave voice to the dream of abundance, where community wealth meant whatever could be shared, not what was stockpiled for oneself (Ajayi, 2024).

The belly-drumming, the music, and the overflowing hospitality became symbols of how laughter and welcome held a village together. In earlier chapters, seasonal rituals and gift-giving festivals showed how sharing kept the world in balance; tanuki tales echoed this spirit, making generosity joyful rather than dutiful. Rhythm and humor did quiet work here: breaking down barriers between rich and poor, newcomer and regular, reminding everyone that the heart of the village beat strongest around a shared table.

**Lucky Bellies & Village Peacemakers**

Images of tanuki with enormous bellies and playful faces line shopfronts and festival gates across Japan. Where some cultures might interpret such exaggeration as mockery or shame, here it signals safety, joy, and good luck. The big belly promises prosperity without stinginess—a merchant who posts a tanuki statue by his door invites neighbors to trust that they'll get fair measure and be treated to a bit of fun along the way. Even the tanuki's famously oversized testicles, while surprising to outsiders, are tokens of fortune, abundance, and cheerfulness, never seen as crude within their context. By placing such figures in daily life, villages reminded themselves that happiness and plenty are found not in perfection, but in cheerful imperfection and honest dealing (Ajayi, 2024).

These visual cues work hand-in-hand with story endings that value harmony above victory. Conflicts in tanuki tales—whether over spilled sake, a missing dumpling, or an insulted official—rarely lead to banishment or defeat. More often, someone apologizes, shares a meal, or donates to the local shrine, repairing bonds for the next day's life together. This pattern shaped listeners' sense of justice: winning means finding ways to continue as neighbors, not scoring points or holding grudges. Those who learn to laugh at themselves, give generously, and seek peace wind up admired, even if they once played the fool. Here, the stories reflect the broader kami tradition of honoring balance, inviting everyone to imagine a world where kindness and wisdom build lasting connections (Ajayi, 2024).

But folklore didn't only teach through laughter and abundance. As tales moved beyond the raucous scenes of shops and taverns, other spirits waited among steep peaks and ancient woods, ready to guide their listeners up paths where resilience, endurance, and the humor of survival would bring new kinds of wisdom.

## Mountain Spirits and Itako Voices

Climbing into the Japanese mountains, each footstep crunches on frozen leaves and loose stone. The air sharpens, colder with every step, while the trees stand like silent guardians. Here, physical challenge and spiritual testing walk hand in hand. Where tanuki stories bring laughter and connection, mountain traditions call on people to steady their minds, find patience, and listen for what lies hidden in the mists. Both humor and hardship have their place; together, they shape a moral landscape where balance matters (Hori, 1975).

Shugendō monks, known as yamabushi—literally "one who lies down in the mountains"—embody this spirit. They rise before dawn in layers of white robes, faces stung by wind. Their rituals stretch from simple river crossings to elaborate fire ceremonies at icy altitudes. These acts are not just exercises in endurance or willpower. Each moment asks them to let go of pride and distraction, echoing earlier tales: like the fox who bends with change, the yamabushi's path is shaped by discipline and humility. Even the stones seem to watch as pilgrims press onward, their focus trained on every uneven surface, every cut of wind. These tough routes teach that wisdom can be born out of hardship shared and obstacles overcome together.

At the peaks, shrines welcome both casual hikers and devoted ascetics. Heartbeats thud in ears after a long climb, and there is a hush broken only by wind or distant bells. Many stop to build a small cairn or whisper a prayer, leaving behind a coin—a tiny gift to the guardian spirits. Even those unfamiliar with local ritual sense something special. When you reach a summit shrine, the altitude isn't only about distance above sea level. It's a reminder of the effort required, the shifting weather, and the closeness of sky and story. Quiet markers line these paths: weathered statues, strings of paper streamers, or wooden signposts inscribed with ancient characters. Each one holds whispers from the past, nods to those who traveled earlier, and hints that your footsteps join a much older dance (Hori, 1975).

In mountain villages or at roadsides, women called itako sit cross-legged before hushed listeners. Often blind and frequently on the social edges, itako are spirit mediums whose voices seem to bridge worlds. Wearing indigo-dyed robes, they beat drums or clap blocks of wood, their chants carrying the names of ancestors over the valleys. One might see an elderly woman cup her hands, calling guidance for families facing a lost harvest or quarreling siblings. The advice arrives wrapped in familiar sayings or practical steps—plant early, forgive first, hold feasts for the dead so memory stays strong. The rituals may feel mysterious, but their purposes are clear: helping people meet fear and confusion with steadiness. In communities shaped by loss or uncertainty, itako are keepers of both story and solution (Hori, 1975). Their presence broadens who has authority to speak for the unseen, bringing

Chapter 5: Tales with Teeth and Tails: Folklore as Cultural Code

women, those living with blindness, and ordinary villagers into the circle of storytellers and guides.

Pilgrim economies knit these mountain traditions into daily life. At dusk, lamp-lit inns serve soups spiced with miso, and tired travelers share muddy boots and stories in common rooms lined with straw mats. Vendors near trailheads offer walking sticks, charms for safe passage, and pickles made from wild greens. Guides point out safe crossings or warn of storm clouds brewing over the next ridge. On festival days, even remote paths hum with visitors, all woven into a network of give-and-take: guides teach songs, guests leave coins, innkeepers send children ahead to fetch water. Hospitality here means more than a warm meal. Everyone joins in keeping the road open, with extra bowls for strangers, fair prices for lost travelers, and shared respect for the slopes. Economy and ritual tiptoe together, each bolstering the other (Hori, 1975).

Book themes echo in these mountains—ritual and everyday action, story and grounded practice. Pilgrimage mirrors old journeys between home and sacred site, weaving individual resolve into communal memory. Every bowl of soup shared, every chant heard across foggy passes, links today's seekers to generations who've trusted the land to teach lessons worth bringing back. What's learned among the peaks returns to villages and towns below: patience, gratitude, and an ethic of help passed from neighbor to neighbor. Just as the fox and tanuki show how to adapt and laugh together, the mountain's wisdom finds its way home—ready for the stories of small heroes waiting around the family hearth (Hori, 1975).

# Children of Wonder: Small Heroes and Big Lessons

While mountain ascetics trained through endurance and spirit mediums channeled ancestral counsel, village hearths hosted another kind of teaching—stories where the smallest figures modeled the largest virtues. In Japanese folklore, children and other humble heroes often stand at the center of adventures that ask more of their heart than of their strength. Take Issun-bōshi, barely an inch tall, who slips between barriers meant to keep out giants, or the tiny animal companions in Momotarō's tale, whose gifts and bravery outmatch fearsome foes. These protagonists navigate a world sized for others by turning constraints into resources. Sliding under doors or riding on the back of a bird, they show how imagination expands where brute force stops. Their victories remind listeners that courage and cleverness matter more than surface appearance, inviting every child—and adult—to see limits as opportunities for creative action.

Tiny bodies slip past locked gates or hide beneath bowls, avoiding dangers that would overwhelm larger warriors. Each time these characters overcome a challenge with wit or kindness, communities watching the fire grow attentive. Resourcefulness isn't just a trait in these tales—it's the heart of survival and belonging. When a hero finds a way forward despite being ignored by the powerful, the story whispers that value isn't handed out by those at the top but claimed by those who persist. Listeners learn to question hierarchies that reward only visible strength, finding inspiration in smallness itself. The image of Issun-bōshi rowing his bowl-canoe down a river suggests that anyone, no matter their size or status, can steer their fate with focus and adaptability.

Gift helpers play a major role in this pattern of growth. Magical animals and spirits are drawn to those who act with unselfconscious kindness. A child frees a trapped mouse without asking for anything in return and later receives enchanted thread that helps untangle trouble. Or a wounded sparrow brings a magical feather after a gentle hand mends its wing. These gifts don't fix everything; they extend the hero's reach just enough to make new choices possible. A flying feather lets the protagonist escape danger—but the path must still be chosen. A length of magic thread binds the villain only if the hero acts bravely. These moments echo the ethic woven through household rituals discussed earlier in the book: reciprocity works best when it comes from caring for others long before help is needed. Just as offerings to house spirits acknowledge gratitude and ongoing relationship, so do folktales reward those who invest in ties with people and nonhuman neighbors alike.

The threefold test structure seen across Japanese stories teaches growth by trial, not by accident or luck. Trials come in threes—a first attempt marked by enthusiasm and failure, a second by reflection and adjustment, and a third earning true success. Here, a small hero tries to carry water up a steep hill, spilling it the first time but learning patience. The next effort brings a clever solution—a leaf folded into a cup—but a misstep still follows. Only on the third try, blending observation, creativity, and steady attention, does the water reach the summit. This rhythm normalizes mistakes as stepping stones, showing audiences that learning happens through practice. In some stories, virtues change with each test: honesty breaks a curse, courage faces a monster, humility opens a closed door. Watching these shifts, listeners see that real growth means trying, failing, and trying again with new insight each time. It encourages not only perseverance but also the ability to reflect and adapt—a skill as useful in daily life as in fairyland.

Homecoming carries rewards deeper than treasure alone. Japanese tales often close with scenes of restoration instead of riches hoarded away. When a little hero returns, celebrations welcome them back but community harmony stands at the center. Fields bloom again, rivers flow where drought once lingered, quarrels end around shared meals, and even the smallest helper—be it a mouse or sparrow—is remembered at the feast. Riches, if given, usually support the whole household or village. The closing scene asks everyone gathered to imagine how they too might share, reconcile, or express thanks. These endings restate the values threaded throughout folk spirituality: gratitude, fairness, and acknowledgment of all who helped along the way. The lesson isn't just about doing good to get ahead. It's about returning with something worth sharing, reinforcing the idea described in ethnographic research that folktales work as potent tools for modeling morality and nurturing reciprocal care, echoing pedagogical patterns found in diverse traditions (Wiysahnyuy & Ngalim Banfegha Valentine, 2023).

These stories serve as a portable code—one that moves beyond the hearth and into classrooms, friendships, and family life. Foxes may test honesty, tanuki puncture pride, mountains teach endurance, and tiny heroes reveal that character, not status, defines belonging. Here, ritual, narrative, and everyday ethics converge, showing readers that meaning doesn't reside only in shrine halls or mountainside pilgrimages. It's lived out in choices both dramatic and quiet, wherever people remember to be clever, patient, and kind. Stepping from folklore into daily life, anyone can become a child of wonder—measuring worth by resolve, generosity, and connection. As the next chapter approaches, material symbols will take up these same values, offering reminders you can hold in your hands, wear on your body, and share with others—each one carrying the wisdom of small heroes and big lessons wherever you go.

## Bringing It All Together

Looking back at these stories, it's clear that animal spirits in Japanese folklore are much more than clever creatures or figures of fear. Foxes, raccoon dogs, and even mountain voices all carry messages about how to act and what values matter. Their tricks, jokes, and tests aren't just entertainment—they're invitations to pay attention, to question our snap judgments, and to remember the power of kindness and humility. These tales gently remind us that wisdom can arrive in many shapes: a tricky fox challenging someone's honesty, a playful tanuki helping people laugh at themselves, or a mountain spirit rewarding endurance and shared effort.

When we approach these characters as cultural teachers instead of just symbols or monsters, the stories open up new layers of meaning. They offer guidance about trust, generosity, and the importance of balance within a community. By stepping into these folktales, we learn not only about Japanese traditions but also about ways to relate to others—across differences, through good times and bad, and between people and the natural world. Each story becomes a mirror, reflecting how we might live with more awareness, care, and joy in our own lives.

# Chapter 6: Signs and Gateways: Material Symbols of the Sacred

On a crisp winter morning in Kyoto, Aiko, a local shopkeeper, found herself pausing at the vibrant vermilion torii of Fushimi Inari. The city's usual hustle faded behind her as she stepped through this striking gateway, leaving the busy street for a sacred path lined by countless gates donated by businesses weathering challenges past. With deliberate care, she replaced the ofuda above her family's kitchen doorway—a small but meaningful ritual to invite protection into their home—and hung an ema bearing her nephew's wishes for success in his upcoming exams. Her journey continued with acts steeped in tradition: rinsing her hands at the purification basin, fastening a fresh shide to a rope near a quiet altar, and scattering salt on her stall counter. Each gesture connected to objects rich with history and intention, subtly transforming everyday spaces into places of mindfulness and thankfulness.

This seamless flow from city street to sanctuary through material symbols offers more than routine; it invites reflection on how physical markers like gates, amulets, and talismans shape our experience of sacredness. Starting here—with the gate that frames entry and signals a shift in presence—we explore how these tangible symbols act as thresholds, crafting spaces that are attentive, protective, and deeply connected to both community stories and personal hopes. Together, these elements create a lived map where ordinary moments become invitations to engage with something larger, quietly guiding visitors like Aiko through rituals of gratitude and care.

## Torii and Threshold Thinking

Aiko pauses at the first vermilion gate, her hands tightening around a bag from an early-morning bakery run. The world is already awake around Fushimi Inari. Taxi engines rumble, bicycles click past, sunlight glances off storefront windows. But at the base of the hill, that simple torii—two upright posts with a straight lintel and secondary crossbar—cuts a crisp line across the path. Its color stands out against green leaves and gray pavement. People slow their pace here almost without knowing why, shifting shopping bags or tucking stray hair behind one ear. A man smooths his jacket, a girl straightens her backpack straps. Some bow, lightly, before stepping forward. This frame doesn't bar entry; instead, it invites attention. Everyday routines adjust as bodies align to this border between ordinary and something else—an encounter that unfolds not through rules but through geometric invitation (Reader, 2008).

Simple forms recalibrate focus by working on the senses. That splash of vivid vermilion isn't only for show; it breaks the monotony of city tones and forest greens, letting visitors

## Chapter 6: Signs and Gateways: Material Symbols of the Sacred

know they have arrived somewhere set apart. The color holds practical value too—the pigments and lacquer help protect wood from rot and repel insects, making the gate last through years of rain and sun (Smyers, 1999). Even in photographs, that sharp red means threshold: a visual pulse calling people to slow down, stand straighter, maybe pay closer attention than they did on the sidewalk. Touching the grain of wood or the rough coolness of stone, feet set more carefully on the path beyond. These gates act as reminders that we move not just through space but through layers of intention, where behavior and awareness begin to change.

Passing beneath one torii feels different from moving through a line of them. At places like Fushimi Inari, rows and arcs of gates stretch into the woods. With each step, shoes shift from gravel to packed earth, the light flickers orange overhead, and temple chatter fades into a hush broken only by wind and crows. Urban noise slips away as footfalls echo softly under the lintels, each gate framing the next—a rhythm that works on both body and mind. Liminality, that sense of being between two worlds, builds one step at a time. Between gates, visitors pause to look up, glance back, or bow again, actions that sharpen the feeling that here, things temporarily work by another logic (Nelson, 2013). Small moments stack together: the press of palms, a shared smile, or whispered greeting. This repetition is not just decoration, but a cue system—a way to train attention so the visitor gradually leaves behind other concerns and becomes part of a quieter procession (Reader, 2008).

Materials cue visitors to the local character of each shrine. Most torii are wooden, some left bare so cedar darkens over seasons, others painted bright vermilion for its protective and symbolic qualities (Smyers, 1999). In places where forests hug the precinct, unpainted wood blends with trunks and leaf shadows, forming gateways that feel both crafted and grown from the land. Stone torii stand heavier and cooler, their weight hinting at endurance and tying the site to hillside or riverside rock. In port towns or market districts, metal gates sometimes rise, gleaming silver or iron-black. Names and dates, carved or painted along the posts, honor the business that funded the construction, the family who prospered enough to donate. These inscriptions turn each torii into a living record of gratitude—part boundary-marker, part community story (Nelson, 2013). When someone stands before a gate and traces kanji cut deep into wood, they see both the present ritual and a timeline of local generosity stretching back generations.

Look up as you pass beneath a torii: the sky appears framed above, clouds moving inside a colored rectangle. The opening pulls the eye upward naturally. Shoulders drop, lungs fill. Whether the view is thick with old cedar branches, distant rooftops, or a glimpse of mountain, the gate turns scenery into stage. Photographers lift their lenses, travelers snap quick shots, and pilgrims close eyes in brief reflection. The lintel edits the outside world, focusing attention outward and inward at once. Standing right there, a visitor chooses to be present—for a wish, a prayer, or a silent moment of thanks (Reader, 2008). Framing sets intention, much as the household kamidana creates a miniature threshold within domestic life or seasonal rites mark turning points across rural landscapes. Moments like these bridge ideas from earlier chapters, showing how the boundaries that shape field, home, and festival also take physical form at the edge of shrine grounds.

Just beyond every torii, smaller thresholds await. Amulets tucked into sleeves, goshuin stamps pressed onto folded paper, strips of white paper tied to branches—all pick up the logic of the gate and carry it forward. What begins at the gate travels with the visitor: a shift in posture, a thread of attention, a small object ready for everyday rituals ahead (Smyers, 1999).

## Amulets, Tablets, and Tokens

Once past the torii's frame, attention sharpens—a new awareness trails with each step into the shrine. Yet that sense of presence doesn't stop at the precinct's edge. In pockets, bags, car mirrors, and doorways, the sacred keeps traveling. Amulets, votive tablets, and talismans extend the shrine's protective touch far beyond its gates, making the relationship with kami a lived experience that adapts to everyday routines.

Omamori—small cloth pouches brimming with blessings—are among the most cherished of these portable tokens. At first touch, an omamori feels both humble and secretive: soft patterned fabric hides the folded paper or wood prayer inside, stitched tightly shut. This design is no accident. The contents are meant to be held, not opened, teaching respect through restraint and heightening their aura. Each omamori carries a precise intention—safe travel, childbirth, business prosperity, academic achievement, traffic safety—often labeled on the pouch in bold characters. Choosing an omamori for someone isn't casual; it's attentive, marking out a life transition or challenge. Imagine a grandmother quietly pressing a study amulet into her grandson's palm before entrance exams, or a colleague clipping a traffic safety charm onto a car mirror. These tokens give form to unspoken care, expressing hope across distance and time (Nelson, 2013). Omamori become companions through journeys, illnesses, interviews, and daily commutes, visible reminders that protection travels with you.

At many shrines, omamori share space with wooden ema—votive plaques that invite visitors' wishes and stories. Writing on an ema brings a private longing into a shared space: prayers for healing, exam victories, new relationships, family peace. People jot down hopes, names, milestones, sometimes a date or drawing, then hang the wooden tablet on racks or wires at the shrine. As the wind stirs, hundreds of plaques tap softly against one another, hinting at the web of wishes linking one person to a wider community. The images on ema anchor individual intentions: horses (for centuries the traditional symbol), zodiac animals, foxes standing guard at Inari shrines, plum blossoms at Tenmangu. Visiting shrines in winter often reveals ema painted with that year's zodiac animal, echoing seasonal rhythms and local identity. Shopkeeper Aiko returns each spring to hang new ema for her nephew, inscribing his wish for courage alongside dozens of others. With every plaque, memory and hope settle into place, rooting personal stories within sacred ground (Reader & Tanabe, 1998).

Ofuda expand the field of protection even further, settling into the intimate spaces of home. Unlike the tucked-away nature of omamori, ofuda are designed for visibility. These rectangular paper or thin wooden talismans come stamped with bright shrine seals or brush-script deity names. After presenting an offering at the shrine, a visitor receives an ofuda to carry back as a mark of continuing guardianship. Proper ritual asks that ofuda be mounted above eye level—often in a kamidana household altar—or fixed above a doorway, forming a subtle but unwavering threshold between daily routines and the unknown outside. Handling ofuda asks for respect and precision: keep them clean, avoid kitchens and bathrooms, change them yearly. Shopkeeper Aiko, after dusting the kamidana, gently exchanges last year's faded ofuda for a fresh one, mindful of both the object's fragility and its weight as a bridge between worlds.

Echoing the seasonal renewal practices we explored in household altars, amulets and talismans also follow a rhythm of return. Once an omamori grows worn or a year's wishes have settled into ema, these objects should never become forgotten clutter. Shrines set out humble boxes near their entrances where people can leave used charms, ema, and ofuda, confident they will be retired with care. Annual burning rituals like Dondoyaki in early January provide closure—a moment when priests thank the objects for their service, offer prayers, and send them into smoke. Watching beloved amulets disappear into the flame, many pause to reflect on challenges faced or joys encountered since their acquisition. Renewal isn't just practical—keeping the material realm tidy—but reflective, inviting gratitude and the courage to move forward (Nelson, 2013).

String, cord, and folded paper seal off the sacred, too. Ema dangle from twisted threads, and ofuda slot into holders crafted with the same care given to shrine ornaments. The next section explores how these ropes and shide papers draw boundaries, create invitation, and maintain the living texture of shrine life.

## Ropes, Papers, and Sacred Craft

Many of the objects we've just explored—amulets, ema, and ofuda—don't simply rest in place or get tucked away. They often hang from twisted ropes or are marked off by strips of folded paper, each element chosen as much for its meaning as its appearance. These boundaries frame tokens and texts, raising daily objects into something that asks for attention. A shimenawa rope, thick and golden, can span the entrance to a shrine or wrap around an ancient tree, holding sacredness close while letting the world see where it begins.

Twist and Fiber: Craft methods encode agricultural heritage
The story of a shimenawa starts in the rice fields. After the harvest, bundles of rice straw or sometimes hemp are gathered, dried, and selected for strength and flexibility. The texture is rough, fibrous, and earthy—it carries the field's

scent even after weaving. Makers twist the fibers to the left, gathering them tightly so no strand slips out. This leftward twist is unmistakeable; run your hand along the rope and you'll feel the way the fibers rise against your palm. Thicker sections signal places of heightened presence—a torii gate or the heart of a ritual ground—while smaller cords may tie around stones or hang over home altars. When tassels are added, they cluster like sheaves of grain, calling the memory of bounty and the promise of protection right into the present. Each rope stands as a physical thread tying the land's power to the spaces set apart for reverence. Even in busy city shrines, the natural fiber and hand-twisted seams speak quietly of rural origins, showing how protection always springs from both the earth and communal labor (efelle creative, 2020).

Lightning Motif: Zigzag papers evoke vitality and presence
Where a boundary needs not just marking but animating, shide zigzag papers appear. Folded from crisp, white washi or modern paper, these strips take on the shape of lightning—or in Japanese, "inazuma." Their sharp pattern recalls a sudden spark across the sky, hinting at energy, purification, and blessing. Hung from shimenawa, tied to wands for rituals, or arranged around temporary holy spaces, shide flutter or snap lightly with wind and movement. The simplicity of the fold matters; careful creases signal respect, and the bright surface shows purity free from defilement. When a breeze runs through a row of shide, the motion brings boundaries to life, reminding anyone who sees them that this isn't a fence but a threshold, alive and watched-over. The visual language is clear: wherever lightning touches, renewal follows. The same

hands that crease shide also carry intention, making visible the belief that attention and care reinforce safety and sanctity (efelle creative, 2020).

Artisans at Work: Seasonal workshops transmit technique
Rope-making is never only about maintenance. Many towns host winter gatherings where caretakers, elders, and curious newcomers meet to replace worn shimenawa before the year turns. Bundles of last season's straw soak in water to soften, then people kneel shoulder-to-shoulder, twisting handfuls together while stories and laughter fill the air. Children learn by copying gestures—how moist a strand should feel, when to tighten, how to tell if the cord is even all the way down. These skills don't live on instruction sheets; they move from hand to hand and voice to ear. As a result, every workshop becomes more than practical upkeep. It's a touchpoint between seasons, a stage for passing on memory, and a simple act that binds generations. When the new rope finally stretches overhead, everyone feels a quiet satisfaction, knowing the line they helped make now stands between the precious inner space and the world outside (efelle creative, 2020).

Repair as Ritual: Mending ropes refreshes relationships
Time always leaves its mark: tassels fray, cords sag or unravel. Instead of seeing wear as loss, caretakers accept it as proof of ongoing work. Small repairs—tying up loose ends, attaching a fresh bow with a whispered word of thanks—keep the outline clear and prevent neglect from creeping in. Every replacement comes with a sense of gratitude, marking both the passage of time and the shared responsibility of keeping the sacred visible. Sometimes, dates of renewal are penned onto tags, or

a small bundle signals a recent refresh. Through these acts, people treat the shimenawa not as a mere object but as a companion in stewardship, cared for out of devotion rather than obligation. Attention and repair signal to the unseen presences—and to one another—that the boundaries still matter. Care cycles back into community, feeding respect for both the place and the powers believed to dwell within (efelle creative, 2020).

These visible boundaries are complemented by cleansing practices—water ladled over hands, salt scattered at thresholds—which serve to prepare both the spaces and those who enter them. The ropes and papers that mark space work together with these rituals to open the way for what is sacred to arrive, guiding us toward the next steps in creating and maintaining places of encounter (efelle creative, 2020).

## Purity, Water, and Salt

While twisted ropes and folded paper mark sacred thresholds, water and salt actively refresh them. They don't simply decorate entrances or hang from rafters; these elements are brought into lived practice to keep the sacred present, making connection a daily act rather than a one-time gesture. The boundaries explored earlier—gates, tokens, ropes—all depend on this ongoing tending, as new dust settles and intentions drift. Purification rituals encourage a return, an attention that is renewed with every approach and each small act.

Stepping toward a shrine, visitors often pause at a temizuya, the low stone basin set beneath a simple roof, filled with clear water. This isn't just about washing away visible dirt. The sequence practiced here—the quiet drawing of water with a ladle, first rinsing the left hand, then the right, raising a scoop to the lips for a light rinse, finally tipping the handle upright so water runs down it—is a choreography of readiness. Cold water against the skin sharpens sensation; the sound of trickling water sets a slower rhythm to breathing and movement. Even when drought leaves basins empty, visitors may mimic these motions in midair, tracing memory more than mechanics. Observers describe this as a quiet conversation between body and place, intention held above perfection (*Harai | Religious Rite*, n.d.).

Salt, too, stands at the edge between worlds. Piled in neat cones beside the doorways of homes and shops, sprinkled before thresholds, or even kept near cash registers, mori-shio signals both protection and welcome. Salt's history as a preserver carries a practical logic: it draws out moisture, halts decay, keeps food safe. In ritual, its meaning widens—it dries up what is stagnant, absorbs what might weigh down the spirit. Sumo wrestlers toss generous handfuls of salt into the ring before matches, a public echo of quieter household gestures. Shops lay out their own pinches before opening for business, not as superstition, but as careful tending of the edge where outside becomes inside. Salt marks the boundary not as a wall, but as a carefully tended edge (*Harai | Religious Rite*, n.d.).

Chapter 6: Signs and Gateways: Material Symbols of the Sacred

Water and salt often travel together, connecting distant landscapes and sacred moments. Coastal communities gather salt from sea spray and tidal pools, carrying its brightness inland to mountain shrines, family altars, and festival sites. Seawater itself, drawn fresh from the shore, blesses spaces far from the coast, a reminder that sacredness flows across boundaries. Rice, salt, and sake make up the core offerings at most shrines—each one an everyday staple, yet made potent by intent. A pinch of coastal salt in a mountain shrine carries the ocean's breadth inland, tying sustenance, land, and blessing into one gesture. These practices echo themes seen in earlier chapters, where rivers and rain signal how nature moves through ritual, making the landscape itself an active partner (*Harai | Religious Rite*, n.d.).

Rain transforms the mood of sacred space. When clouds release gentle showers or sudden downpours, paths darken, wood gleams, stone grows slick beneath cautious feet. Scent rises off earth and cedar. Visitors slow down, pausing under eaves, listening to the steady drumming of rain on tiled roofs and the hush it brings to movement. Rain is never viewed simply as inconvenience; instead, weather invites humility and patience. Unfurling an umbrella or waiting for a break becomes a small practice in itself, modeled on the values embedded in purification. Rain sharpens the senses, heightening awareness of texture, sound, and breath—making presence a lived response to change (*Harai | Religious Rite*, n.d.).

Together, these material symbols create a curriculum of care. Crossing beneath a torii, carrying amulets and wards, tying rope around sacred trees, and quietly rinsing hands at stone basins—all these actions work together, each training attention in its own way. Gates frame entry, tokens carry wishes and protection, ropes remind us of boundaries, and water and salt refresh intention. Each gesture—crossing, carrying, tying, rinsing—trains us to notice thresholds and tend them with care. This vocabulary of materials does more than separate sacred from ordinary; it teaches how to move in the world with grateful mindfulness, preparing us to step into the living choreography of performance and procession ahead (*Harai | Religious Rite*, n.d.).

## Bringing It All Together

Walking with Aiko through the rows of vermilion gates and sharing her simple rituals, we see how these everyday objects and gestures shape more than just sacred sites—they quietly influence the way people move, notice, and connect. The torii marks a shift in rhythm, while amulets, ema, and ofuda keep protection and intention close at hand. Ropes and shide, salt and water, each invite us to care for boundaries, both visible and invisible, drawing attention to what is easily missed in daily life. Every small act—a bow, a tied string, a handful of salt—helps ordinary places feel more attentive and secure.

All these moments add up to something lasting: a living map built on gratitude, presence, and quiet stewardship. Whether stepping under temple gates or leaving a pinch of salt at the shop door, people create links between home, work,

Chapter 6: Signs and Gateways: Material Symbols of the Sacred

community, and spirit. The power of these spaces lies not in grand gestures, but in the layers of care and meaning woven through routine. As we trace these maps for ourselves, we start to see how rituals can transform our own days, welcoming both the known and the mysterious with open eyes and steady hands.

# Chapter 7: Performance and Procession: Movement as Story

Long ago, in the elegant courts of the Heian period, a dance called kagura began as a refined art form where myths were transformed into precise, graceful movements. These performances weren't just entertainment; they told important stories through carefully arranged steps and gestures. Meanwhile, far from the palace, mountain villages took these same tales and wove them into their own seasonal ceremonies, syncing the rhythms of the dances with harvest cycles and local customs. As time passed, the bustling cities of Edo grew these traditions into grand street festivals filled with towering floats, vibrant drum groups, and spirited chants that invited whole neighborhoods to become living temples on the move.

After shifts brought by political reforms and societal changes, including the Meiji era's impact on shrines, these festivals and sacred dances found new life in postwar Japan, reawakening regional pride and cultural memory. Movement—whether delicately performed on a stage or carried forward through crowded streets—has served as a lasting vessel for myth and blessing. This chapter will explore how these kinetic stories have traveled through centuries, starting with the expressive language of kagura and unfolding into the broader landscape of communal performance and procession.

## Kagura and Sacred Dance

Long before kagura became a celebrated part of village festivals, it belonged to courtly displays—stately movements, measured rhythms, and elegant forms designed for imperial audiences. Over time, these sacred dances left palatial confines and took root in the heart of rural communities, adopting local textures and meanings as villagers adapted ancient forms to their own hands and bodies. Kagura remains a living bridge between mythic stories and present-day gatherings, where movement is more than art—it becomes the language through which people remember, retell, and renew their relationship with unseen presences.

Building on our earlier exploration of kami as relational powers, kagura transforms cosmological tales into sequences of gesture and rhythm. Common episodes drawn from Japanese mythology—such as the opening of the cave by the sun goddess or the jubilant return of light—are woven into dance patterns. When a dancer adopts slow, enclosed steps, arms curling inward with a fan partially hiding the face, this often signals a moment of concealment or mourning. The sudden flourish of an open fan, paired with outward-turning steps and sweeping arcs across the stage, marks a joyful revelation or divine emergence. Props like fans stand for wind or change, sakaki branches held upright define sacred boundaries, and mirror-like discs capture the audience's focus just as they once lured hidden deities. Each object functions as punctuation, shaping the story even for those unfamiliar with the details (Nelson, 1996).

The choreography moves in patterns of repetition and surprise, much like musical refrains that help listeners anticipate key moments. Many kagura performances use verse-and-chorus structures, blending recognizable motifs with subtle changes—just as a familiar melody might return in a film score to cue emotion or signal a turning point. This guiding rhythm means that every observer, whether attending their tenth festival or their first, finds orientation points in the unfolding narrative. Children watch for the moment when the hidden dancer bursts forth; elders nod along with gestures they learned decades ago. These shared cues transform the ritual from spectacle to communal storytelling, accessible and open-ended (Thornbury, 1997).

Masks and codified gestures form a visual vocabulary, letting dancers communicate identity, intent, and feeling without words. Masks carved with serene features embody peaceful deities, while sharply defined brows and bared teeth express anger or protectiveness. When a masked performer slowly tilts their head or angles it away, meaning shifts—from respect to warning in a heartbeat. Hand gestures work as visual verbs: circling motions suggest searching, the crisp flick of a folded fan invites blessings or clears obstacles, and forceful stamps anchor sacred space. Even footwork carries meaning—deliberate heel strikes can ward off harm, while nimble side-steps hint at trickster spirits weaving through mortal affairs.

## Chapter 7: Performance and Procession: Movement as Story

Not all performers hide behind masks. Alternating between masked and unmasked roles lets observers see when someone acts as a vessel—a body for the kami to move through—versus when they participate as a celebrant. This shifting boundary helps frame each passage: a masked figure bows low to receive offerings, while an unmasked musician meets the eyes of the community, rooting the scene in shared reality. Watching closely, one learns to read the difference in posture, gaze, and energy, understanding not just who is being played but what is being invoked (Kataoka, 2020).

Performance styles do not travel unchanged. They pick up inflections from landscape, livelihood, and historical memory. In fishing villages, kagura sometimes weaves net-casting or oar-pulling gestures into dances that retell creation myths— local labor folded into celestial drama. Mountain settlements favor heavy stamping beats and layered costumes that echo winter's chill and rocky slopes. Lyrics adapt too, with names of local peaks or rivers sung alongside heaven's deities, rooting universal stories in lived terrain. These performance patterns will echo later when we examine regional craft lineages, showing how place shapes not only guardian spirits but also the way stories are retold over time.

Apprenticeship keeps these traditions alive, not through books, but through bodies—hands learning from hands, feet matching drumbeats under practiced eyes. Young dancers start at the side, carrying instruments and props, absorbing timing and shape until every motion feels natural. Elder mentors give corrections in the form of touch, breath count, or a sharp tap in rehearsal, folding newcomers into rhythm without ever writing steps down. Dancing in annual rites is seen not as entertainment but as service, letting the story and its blessings flow through the community once more. The sense of duty runs deep: each performance is a gift both received and renewed, anchored in memory, trust, and gratitude (Hoff, 2017).

Kagura does not stay confined to the stage. As festival seasons swell, these patterns of embodied prayer spill into the streets—processions and portable shrines carrying stories and blessings into every corner of village life.

## Processions, Floats, and Shared Steps

While kagura performances concentrate myth within the ritual stage, street processions expand these narratives into the shared spaces of everyday life. The same stories that kagura dancers embody through masks and measured steps now travel through neighborhoods on shoulders and carried by hundreds of feet. Where kagura relies on a select group of trained performers, processions bring festival meaning outward—making entire communities both storytellers and participants (Nelson, 1996).

Route choreography gives each procession a living structure shaped by memory and geography. Processional paths rarely follow straight lines; instead, they wind along ancient routes, pause at bridges over rivers, and turn at wells believed to house protective spirits. These pauses are charged moments.

## Chapter 7: Performance and Procession: Movement as Story

When carriers reach the stone bridge at the edge of the old quarter, they stop, turn the float so it faces upstream where people believe a water deity waits, and the lead drummer strikes three slow, echoing beats before the group moves forward again. At crossroads, participants might bow toward a marker wrapped in shimenawa—a rope of straw signaling a sacred boundary—or circle an old tree whose thick trunk bristles with folded paper charms. Each move acknowledges ties between people, land, and unseen protectors. Stopping points help the group reset both physically and ritually; sweat is wiped away, breaths deepen, but eyes stay on the holy object.

Floats act as moving storybooks, their sides crowded with carved panels, painted scenes, and layers of trailing fabric that speak to anyone who looks closely. A young child perched on her father's shoulders points out a fox with sharp ears worked into one side, whispering that it's Inari's messenger. Grandmothers in folding chairs compare the deep blue cloths draped from the top tier—indigo for early summer—against memories of past festivals. Sometimes the float's lower border is lacquered in bright gold, reflecting sunlight onto the street and bringing attention to repairs after recent floods. Each surface teaches what matters here: route stories, the guardian animals of this place, the struggles and harvests that shape lives. One float begins with its base showing the legendary founder crossing a river, climbs upward in scenes of rice planting and first fruits, and ends beneath a painted crane—said to have warned villagers of rising waters. These images need no words and can be read by anyone, turning the float into both an archive and a teacher (Reader & Tanabe, 1998).

Chants organize bodies and open space for collective energy. Simple, repeated calls—shouted by those carrying the mikoshi or portable shrine—signal when to lift, set down, or change pace. 'Wasshoi! Wasshoi!' echoes up and down the line. When the leader calls, hundreds respond together, their voices reaching windows above shops and drawing neighbors to doorways. These calls serve more than just coordination. The beat and volume help the group carry weight safely through tight alleys. Spectators cannot help but echo the cry, joining as companions instead of distant watchers. Rhythms shift slightly with local traditions—some towns draw out syllables, others add clapped reply patterns—so each festival hallmarks itself in sound as well as sight. Chants turn a crowd into a chorus, blending effort and praise with every step taken under sun or rain (Nelson, 1996).

Resting stations punctuate the route, offering both care and reverence. Volunteers gather under blue tarps near the school gate, ready with cool ladles of water and tiny dishes of salt—the gifts refresh bodies and recall purification rites. Here, musicians put aside drums and flutes, letting their hands rest while new carriers linger nearby. The next team bows low before the float, gripping poles with fresh determination. Shade is as valued as any ritual blessing, and a tray of peeled oranges or cups of barley tea pass quickly along the waiting line. This cycle of support keeps both the ceremony and its people strong. These shared pauses remind everyone that sustaining sacred work means sharing practical burdens too.

These chants work in concert with drums and bells to bind time and movement together. The rhythmic calls that coordinate carriers also prepare us to understand how percussion and melody run alongside footfalls. Soon, we will listen more closely—not only to the spoken cheers, but to the full soundscape that moves with the sacred procession (Nelson, 1996).

## Soundscapes of the Sacred

The routes and pauses you encountered in festival processions gain their rhythm through sound. A drum's low beat grounds your steps, echoing like a heartbeat at a measured walking pace. This pulse does more than keep time—it anchors each carrier, tying feet to soil and shared intent. Large taiko drums often set this pace; their deep resonance travels through bodies and town streets alike, letting people feel alignment not just with one another but with the larger flow of the event itself. When movement pauses—at crossroads or sacred sites—the music shifts. The roll of smaller shime-daiko or sharp clack of wooden blocks signals attention, bringing everyone into focus. Rising rolls quicken collective energy before dramatic reveals: a dancer emerges, a float turns, a mask lifts. In these moments, percussion is not only a tool for timing but an emotional conductor, shaping how anticipation or relief washes through the crowd (Montagu, 2017).

Call-and-ground textures fill the air as multiple layers overlap. Big drums lay down the steady foundation that holds the group together, while smaller drums weave intricate patterns across it. Think of the way a bass line supports a song while melody lines dart above—that relationship helps even first-time listeners catch on. Chants ripple through ranks of mikoshi-bearers, syncing breath and muscle. Leaders call, carriers respond, and the cycle repeats until voices blend into one living instrument. These musical cues transform every curve of the procession route into part of the story, using rhythm to shape both space and narrative.

Melody brings memory into play. Simple tunes, built from five-note pentatonic scales, wrap easily around the tongue and mind. Children hum the main festival refrain almost before they understand its meaning. Melodic fragments act like character themes in familiar film scores—a flute motif signals the fox spirit, a descending line hints that the mountain god is near. Fue flutes and kagura-bue pipes thread clear notes through percussion's thick canvas. These melodic bits create hooks that catch and hold the stories being enacted. Through countless repetitions at annual gatherings, melodies turn complex myth into living, shareable knowledge, persisting well beyond the moment words fade from lips (Montagu, 2017).

Just as seasonal rites align labor with lunar cycles, percussion aligns bodies with ritual time. The clang of shrine bells at New Year echoes the agricultural rhythms you heard about earlier, marking boundaries between old and new, sacred and everyday. Bell strikes frame ritual time like clear punctuation. One resonant ring opens the gateway, drawing a hush as all eyes and ears recalibrate. Clusters of suzu bells shimmer through ambient noise when offerings are made or gates swing open, focusing attention on sacred action. As the last tone fades, daily life seeps back in gently, never snapping the spell but dissolving it softly. Bells become sonic liminal spaces, doorways everyone can recognize even at a distance (Montagu, 2017).

Silence shapes the soundscape as much as drums or bells. Planned hushes before major reveals heighten the senses—a brief suspension where breath becomes audible, hearts seem louder, and anticipation tightens. During slow turns on narrow lanes, chanting may stop so carrier footfalls and quiet breaths mark each step. This pause isn't empty; it re-centers focus, allowing ritual depth to settle in. At the end, instead of applause, a gentle quiet lingers, giving emotion and memory room to take root. Silence works like negative space in painting, framing what came before and inviting interpretation after. Recognizing such silences helps listeners grow sensitive to structure—these are intentional choices, not simple gaps.

From sound and timing, we turn to the materials and bodies that make these stories visible and felt. Ears have carried you through movement's temporal framework; now eyes and hands will reveal how costume, prop, and endurance bring devotion to life in shapes you can see and touch.

## Costume, Craft, and Embodiment

As the sound of drums and bells sets the pace for processions and performances, it is the vibrant sight of costumes and masks that marks sacred presence. While sonic patterns draw everyone into ritual time, fabric, wood, and pigments bring ritual figures to life before onlookers' eyes. Performers slip into carefully assembled layers, transforming themselves into visible vessels for tradition. Every fold of cloth, brushstroke of pigment, and cut of wood carries meaning passed through hands and hearts across generations (Johnson, 2025).

Textile choices in these performances function as a coded language. Patterns woven or embroidered into garments often echo sacred geography: mountain spirits will be robed in pine-needle motifs, fox messengers may wear sashes with running water or rice sheaf embroidery. These visual cues guide the audience, helping them read roles—just as earlier we saw how tree and stone markers reveal kami presences in the land. White silk robes commonly signal purity during purification rites, while bold crimson linings hint at vitality and protection. A shrine maiden dressed in glowing white and gold seems to move with the dawn itself, whereas deep indigo brocades clothe guardian figures, combining the depth of night with the promise of watchfulness. Garments shift with the seasons, too. Summer brings flowing white hemp or silk, cool to the touch and light enough for dancing in open air. Winter

## Chapter 7: Performance and Procession: Movement as Story

festivals call for rich brocades, their weight warming the body as they catch the flicker of lanterns. The fabric's heft or delicacy mirrors the turn of the agricultural year—cotton thin as morning mist for spring sowing rituals, padded silks for winter's long vigils.

Masks make emotion and spirit both visible and tangible. Carvers select woods such as cypress, known for its strength and surprising lightness, or paulownia, which balances durability with ease of movement. The choice is never only practical; each timber carries history, scent, and a sense of place. Skilled hands shape brow, cheek, and mouth so expressions can leap across the distance between stage and crowd. A mask might carry a sly smile that brightens in torchlight or a frown deepening into shadow as incense curls skyward. Pigments ground from mineral earths—reds, whites, soot blacks—are mixed with natural binders like sap or egg yolk, a process blending artistry with ritual care (Johnson, 2025). Color holds power here: red might speak of life force, black of mystery, white of transition or endurance. Lacquer seals everything in a gloss that both protects and draws out the carved lines, turning the mask into an artifact that flashes with every twist of the head.

Wearing these garments and masks demands real effort. Layered robes can weigh more than fifteen pounds, and towering headdresses require practice simply to balance, let alone dance. Ropes and sashes tied around the waist or shoulders help share the load, letting performers pace each step for ceremony rather than speed. During a summer matsuri, sweat gathers beneath collars, and breath grows careful—each movement slowed not just by the costume's weight, but by awareness of being watched, honored, and, sometimes, possessed by the spirit one represents. Spectators learn to see the labor in the subtle control of motion, the steadying clasp of a fan, the quiet breaths taken between songs. Physical strain becomes another kind of offering, making devotion visible—an echo of shared community tasks like village planting or harvests, where effort knits people and place together.

Care for all these materials continues well beyond performance day. Robes are aired out at the change of seasons, folded along set creases, stored with cedar slats or fragrant leaves to ward off insects. Ritual phrases accompany the unveiling and packing away of masks, treating them not as simple tools but as honored guests who return home after work is done. Some families keep detailed records in ink: who mended a sleeve, who replaced a threadbare sash, who repainted a fading eyelid. These logs trace craft lineages—reminders that behind every costume stands a web of human hands and memory. The devotion given to mask storage recalls the ancestral altar tending described in earlier chapters, where household objects become bridges between past and present.

What emerges is a living tradition. Each robe lifted onto shoulders, each mask fitted over a face, links today's performance with centuries of story and stewardship. The care lavished in making and maintaining these objects ripples forward, connecting festive gatherings with sacred forests, old tales with new voices. As later chapters will show, every region shapes this care differently, blending histories into lineages that audiences can learn to recognize, respect, and even support. Through material presence and embodied ritual, story finds a way to live on—in wood, in fabric, and in the lives that carry them. (Johnson, 2025)

## Bringing It All Together

Looking back on the stories and traditions explored in this chapter, it's clear that movement plays a special role in connecting people to myth, memory, and each other. Whether through the elegant steps of kagura at court or the lively processions winding through city streets, dance and ritual have always been about more than performance—they are living languages that carry history, blessing, and identity to every corner of a community. The floats, costumes, music, and chants all work together, letting everyone—performers and bystanders alike—take part in something bigger than themselves. Even as customs shift from palace to village, then to bustling neighborhoods, the heart of these traditions remains the same: sharing stories in ways that can be seen, felt, and remembered.

Today, these festivals and dances still shape how people relate to their local places and shared pasts. Every mask carved, every robe folded away with care, keeps the connection between old tales and new generations alive. Through movement, sound, and craft, communities keep finding ways to turn everyday spaces into sacred ones, if only for an afternoon or a season. It's in these moments—dancing shoulder-to-shoulder, listening for a drumbeat, watching a procession wind past—that old wisdom slips quietly into the present, inviting us all to join in the ongoing story.

# Chapter 8: Blended Paths: Syncretism, Doctrine, and Local Practice

Have you ever noticed how certain places and rituals in Japan bring together the sacred in unexpected ways? Imagine walking through a quiet shrine where bright red gates welcome you, while nearby, the scent of burning incense hints at Buddhist prayers. These sites don't just happen to share space; they tell a story of traditions woven tightly together over centuries. This chapter invites you to think about those threads — how kami, the local spirits cherished in Shinto, and elements of Buddhist belief entwined to become something new and deeply meaningful for communities. It's like watching a fabric being stitched and unstiched repeatedly, never quite coming apart despite efforts to separate the parts.

Starting from the history of Shinbutsu Shugo, the blending of kami worship and Buddhist practice, we'll explore the ways these spiritual paths joined and then split, showing how everyday people helped keep the bonds alive. Even when laws tried to pull traditions apart, daily life continued weaving them back together through festivals, family rituals, and stories passed down at kitchen tables. The journey ahead will uncover how shared devotion shaped not just religious sites, but the rhythms of ordinary lives — a living blend that offers insight into how culture adapts and survives across time.

## Shinbutsu Shugo: Entwined Traditions

You've met the torii gates, household altars, and seasonal festivals that shape everyday life in Japanese homes and communities. You've walked through sacred groves and listened to folk stories where local spirits, or kami, appear almost as family. Yet, turning a corner, you might find yourself in a spot where monks chant sutras or incense burns before a statue of the Buddha. What happens when you realize that many sites, objects, and practices bear signs of both traditions? This chapter invites you to set aside tidy labels and step into the intricate world of Shinbutsu Shugo—the blending of kami veneration and Buddhist practice that defined centuries of spiritual life in Japan (Shinto & Shintoism Guidebook, Guide to Japanese Shinto Deities (Kami), Shrines, and Religious Concepts, n.d.; Jann, 2022). Rather than being locked in conflict, these ways of honoring the unseen often expanded side by side, sometimes merging so fully that people experienced no boundary at all.

In this landscape of exchange, Japanese communities found meaning by linking local kami with Buddhist figures. The underlying logic was simple and generous: kami were both protectors and seekers—they guarded fields and forests, but they could also be guided by Buddhist teachings. Buddhist monks explained that powerful bodhisattvas like Kannon, known for compassion, might choose to reveal themselves as a village's water deity, ensuring safe harvests for those who performed rituals at both shrine and temple. In return, villagers honored the kami with offerings and asked for blessings, then joined Buddhist memorial services to help restless spirits reach enlightenment. Each group gained from the other: kami kept temples free from calamity, while Buddhist rituals offered peace to the restless or angry spirits that might trouble a temple's grounds (Shinto & Shintoism Guidebook, n.d.; Jann, 2022). This reciprocity made sense for people who wanted protection in this life and comfort for ancestors in the next. Most didn't puzzle over technical ideas like "original ground and manifest trace"—they simply saw their divine guardians working together.

If you visited one of these shared spaces, the scene could feel both familiar and surprising. You might pass under a bright red torii arch, symbolizing the entrance to sacred space. After rinsing your hands at the water basin—to purify body and mind—you'd hear the slow ring of a bell come from a temple hall just beyond the camphor trees. Chapter 2 described sacred groves; here, those trees shaded both a Shinto shrine and a Buddhist temple, their roots entwined beneath carefully raked gravel. Sometimes, a single structure held both a Buddhist altar and sacred ropes reserved for kami worship, echoing Chapter 6's material symbols that carried overlapping meanings. Preservation felt practical: villages pooled money and effort for repairs, split between priest and monk, ensuring neither shrine nor temple fell into neglect. Pilgrims walked routes that tied several shrines and temples together, offering prayers and coins at each stop (Shinto & Shintoism Guidebook, n.d.).

Teaching tools helped people grasp these relationships without needing theology. Imagine a painted scroll showing the sun shining behind a mountain—one light, two forms. In this analogy, a Buddhist figure is the great sun; the kami are its rays reaching down to warm the earth. A grandmother might reassure her grandchild that both Kannon and the local spring's kami watch over their well, inviting requests for safe water and guidance with equal confidence. Artists reinforced these links visually—a statue of a kami might wear a Buddhist halo, or temple mandalas would include shrine rope motifs. These images showed gods and buddhas not as rivals, but as partners, making the experience of devotion fuller and more immediate.

Festivals and ceremonies brought this mixture to life in lively, colorful displays. On festival days, ornate mikoshi—portable kami shrines—paraded alongside Buddhist banners, accompanied by drummers whose beats mingled with the deep intonation of monks chanting sutras. In one part of the procession, a Shinto priest purified the way with waving branches, while just steps away, a Buddhist monk recited prayers for departed souls. Neither role seemed out of place—instead, both were welcomed as natural parts of community celebration. Seasonal events, especially those marking planting or harvest, became occasions for joint prayer and ritual exchange: thanking the gods for bounty and remembering ancestors together, expressions woven into the fabric of daily life (Jann, 2022). This flexible coexistence would face profound challenges as new policies tried to draw sharper lines between traditions—a topic waiting just ahead.

## Meiji Separation and Its Ripples

The collaborative arrangements described earlier faced sudden upheaval when the Meiji government introduced new policies that restructured the religious landscape of Japan. Centuries of shared sites, ritual exchange, and paired icons were disrupted as laws enforced a sharp boundary between what had often developed organically: Shinto and Buddhist traditions (Shizuka, 2023). Temples that once housed kami shrines, and shrines that welcomed Buddhist rituals, now stood on opposite sides of an administrative line. Priests found their roles redefined—not by gradual community consensus but by legal edict. Where once a single document listed both shrine and temple events, officials updated registries, creating separate ledgers for each institution. Signboards outside sacred sites now displayed revised names, sometimes omitting Buddhist or Shinto references altogether. A local school textbook that once taught about harmonized spiritual guardians began to focus instead on civic duty and reverence for the emperor, reflecting pressure from above rather than community practice.

Edicts went beyond paperwork. Material changes transformed the very shape and appearance of religious life.

Officials ordered the relocation of Buddhist statues that had stood inside Shinto precincts, moving them out of sight or into storage. Shrine implements—drums, bells, banners—no longer mingled with temple offerings. Red torii gates received fresh coats of paint and new emblems, while alcoves once filled with Buddha images sat empty. Paths that wound through both shrine groves and temple gardens were rerouted, sometimes blocked off by fences, so that worshippers could not easily visit both on the same journey. Auxiliary halls that formerly hosted joint festivals or seasonal rites were reassigned or dismantled, and visitors noticed the changed rhythm of communal gatherings. These shifts made separation a tangible, visible experience. Across Japan, some regions witnessed the near-erasure of Buddhist landmarks as a wave of anti-Buddhist violence destroyed temples and ousted priests, leaving blank spaces where familiar structures stood before (Shizuka, 2023).

These material alterations came with narrative reframing. Records were edited and official histories rewritten to emphasize pure lineages. Guidebooks that once described the interplay of kami and buddhas began speaking only of one tradition per site, erasing the record of centuries of collaboration. Festivals that drew everyone together under wide banners became tagged as either agricultural celebrations or memorial services, pressed into new categories to fit the legal system. In villages, elders adjusted their stories, highlighting those aspects that fit the fresh frameworks while letting other details slip into silence. This was not always outright denial; often it was a quiet shift of

## Chapter 8: Blended Paths: Syncretism, Doctrine, and Local Practice

emphasis, a way to meet new expectations while quietly holding memory close. The book's broader theme—how place-based practice endures in the face of outside change—echoes here, as communities balanced compliance with preservation of their own rhythms. Adaptation did not mean forgetting, and even as tales shifted, fragments of blended tradition lived in private conversations and remembered routes.

Yet beneath these official reconfigurations, everyday devotion continued almost as before. In many homes, family altars still hosted both Buddhist sutras and shrine talismans. Grandparents placed offerings at both a temple incense burner and the small kamidana shelf above the door. People scheduled visits to nearby shrines for harvest rites and then stopped at the temple to remember ancestors, following patterns set long before any decree. Children learned deity nicknames that combined Buddhist and Shinto terms, evidence of old habits running beneath new rules. Pilgrimage routes survived in secret or simply went unremarked, as neighbors accompanied each other to paired sites each year. Language itself preserved connections, with prayers that wove together references and blessings from both lines. These actions were not acts of protest but practical continuities, born from affection, convenience, or simple habit. Official registries might mark a household as Buddhist or Shinto, but lived faith rarely settled into such clear divisions (Ravitch, n.d.; Shizuka, 2023).

This gap between official categories and household altars shapes what comes next. While authorities revised records and rituals, community memory and daily devotion created space for persistent blending. The following section will explore how these unwritten practices resisted easy classification, carrying the old harmony forward despite everything that changed.

## Local Orthodoxy vs. Lived Practice

Despite formal divisions imposed during the Meiji period, daily life often moved to its own beat. While registries and public ceremonies reflected efforts to categorize faith—Shinto here, Buddhism there—households and communities quietly exercised their own judgment, blending traditions at home altars, in local festivals, and out in the fields. Textbook teachings about how to perform a norito (Shinto prayer) or recite a Buddhist sutra offered clear instructions, but families frequently adapted these scripts. A grandmother might begin with the "correct" phrase, then add an extra refrain her own mother whispered long ago, believing it would bring extra luck in the new year. This layering of official and inherited was less an act of resistance than one of affection and continuity.

Written prescriptions for practice only went so far. Local priests and monks taught from approved manuals, but people adjusted rituals to fit family stories, dialects, and memories. In many villages, chant melodies drifted gently from their standard patterns, bending to include regional scales or childhood songs that made children smile and join in. Where temples and shrines stood side by side, neighbors borrowed

## Chapter 8: Blended Paths: Syncretism, Doctrine, and Local Practice

stands meant for one kind of offering and repurposed them for both rice cakes and incense, showing respect with what they had on hand. The seasonal harvest festival, described as a Shinto rite in theory, sometimes grew into a joint event: half-day prayers at the local shrine, then a procession stopping to honor ancestors at a Buddhist altar under a cherry tree—all stitched together by laughter, shared food, and a sense that everyone belonged. Remember the household altars we explored earlier in Chapter 3; here, kamidana (Shinto shelf) and butsudan (Buddhist cabinet) were often tucked into the same alcove, or separated only by the day's needs—rice for the kami in the morning, flowers for the ancestors at night. These gentle improvisations made doctrine feel alive, rooted in a web of family and place rather than distant rules.

Ritual timing, too, bent to meet real-world necessities. Weather shaped everything. If heavy rains washed out mountain trails, pilgrimage dates shifted without shame, ritual purity making way for safe passage. Families in fishing villages followed tide charts more closely than calendars. Dawn prayers moved with the moon; ceremonies delayed until nets were hauled in and families reunited on-shore. Farmers facing an early monsoon brought offerings forward by a week, trusting the spirits cared more for their intent and wellbeing than for perfect adherence to schedules. The seasonal flexibility seen in Chapter 4 comes through even stronger now, as survival and gratitude intertwine. Rather than betraying tradition, such responses mirror centuries-old wisdom found in Indigenous practices worldwide, where local knowledge and spiritual methods blend to foster harmony and resilience within communities (Gede et al., 2024; McKinley, 2023).

In the privacy of the home, adaptation took on uniquely gentle forms. A family places a travel charm—blessed by a priest—next to ancestor tablets in the butsudan before a child leaves for school, tying hopes for safety to both Buddhist and Shinto guardians. Parents, trying to keep evening prayers lively after dinner, shorten recitations or swap a formal chant for a favorite folksong. Children clap twice at the little kamidana before running outside to play, following a rhythm picked up from an older sibling rather than prescribed order. For caregivers tending to elders, devotional routines merge with acts of care—incense is lit when it's time for medication, turning each gesture into both blessing and reminder. These small choices infuse old forms with warmth and relevance. The household scenes from Chapter 3 return here not as static images, but as living spaces where adaptation is remembered and reinvented every day.

Stories do the quiet work of keeping all this possible. In both rural towns and city neighborhoods, folktales and local legends set the pattern for what feels right. A story about a river spirit who resolves quarrels becomes the model for how friends make up after a disagreement—a box of sweets exchanged at the footbridge, a whispered apology carried by the current. During Obon, tales of ancestral ghosts drifting home on lantern-light turn into concrete advice: speak softly near water, leave fruit and tea at crossroads, mind your steps in the dark. These stories carry more authority than printed instructions from distant authorities because they are lived, retold, and felt. The tale of a traveling monk inviting a mountain kami along his path becomes the reason a family visits both temple and shrine on the same holiday. Folklore, like song, memory, and weather, shapes daily choices, letting families honor rules while embracing lived meaning. Through narrative, adaptation becomes not just permitted but expected, ensuring that sacred practice remains close to those who need it most.

## Reading Syncretism with Care

Building on these examples of everyday adaptation, where families and villages quietly mix elements from Shinto and Buddhism regardless of official policies, readers stand at the point where insight into syncretism becomes a practical tool for respectful engagement. Seeing how lived traditions adapt to community needs lays the groundwork for a deeper way of reading local practice.

### Avoid Purity Myths

When approaching historical sites or contemporary rituals, don't assume that any "authentic" tradition is untouched or unmixed. Even temples and shrines that look separate today often share roots in centuries-old compounds, where priests and laypeople moved easily between Buddhist and kami veneration. Famous examples include complexes like

Tōshōgū, which blended both lineages until forced separation measures, and countless rural shrines where Buddhist bells still hang beside the torii gates (2023). Many festivals draw on both Buddhist sutras and Shinto purification—not because anyone ignored true doctrine, but because communities found ways to make meaning together. Even language itself absorbed new flavors: terms like "gongen" (a kami understood as a Buddha's temporary manifestation) show how conversation wove different philosophies into everyday speech (Khan Academy, 2018; 2023). Mixture isn't about loss—it's about creative problem-solving, letting traditions respond to real lives instead of abstract ideals.

**Trace Layers: Practice as Investigation**

Every shrine path or temple garden holds visible traces of blending for those who know what to look for. Start by noticing architecture—look for a lotus finial perched atop a typically Shinto roofline, or an inscription written half in classical Chinese (used in Buddhism) and half in native syllabary (used in many norito, or ritual prayers). Buddhist roof tiles might appear on buildings called jingū, while the presence of vermilion gates may mark even a temple precinct. Next, listen closely during ceremonies. You might hear a norito recited, only to be followed by a chant in Sanskrit or Chinese—a living blend that marks out layers of history. Pay attention to vocabulary: names ending in "-ji" flag Buddhist origin, while those ending in "-jinja" or "-sha" point to Shinto. Ask questions gently to those who carry these practices forward. Instead of demanding origins, try, "When did this part of the festival change?" or, "Has this prayer always sounded like this?" These detective skills turn every visit into an adventure, helping you follow the threads running through the cultural fabric (2023; Khan Academy, 2018).

**Listen Locally: Centering Community Wisdom**

What you see in books or pamphlets offers only one layer of truth. The people tending altars, sweeping grounds, or remembering old festival routes carry knowledge that textbooks can't capture. Engage with local experts, elders, and participants as fellow learners, not as extractors of data. When you attend a ceremony or join a celebration, notice where families pause, which songs move elders to tears, or what objects children are taught never to touch. Printed guides may hint at history, but their real value lies in starting conversations. Before photographing or writing about someone's story, ask permission and offer to share your impressions afterward, crediting the source of your learning. Documenting responsibly turns observation into partnership—and honors the labor behind each tradition's survival (2023; Khan Academy, 2018).

**Hold Complexity: Leaning Into Both/And**

A single gesture, like lighting incense at a home altar, rarely carries just one meaning. It's common for the same action to honor ancestors, express gratitude, and call on protective forces, all depending on context and intent. Doctrinal explanations—Buddhist merit transfer, for example—sit alongside folk understandings and personal memories. Rather than choosing between them, practice thinking in "both/and" terms: this moment is both a Buddhist act and a family memory; this prayer uses both ancient formula and local improvisation; this legend means one thing to the head priest and quite another to the teenagers carrying the mikoshi (portable shrine). Whenever you write or think about a practice, name whose voice you're presenting and leave room for other readings. This approach reflects the interpretive humility introduced in Chapter 1 and will matter even more in coming chapters, as you meet stories carried differently across regions, generations, and changing times.

The interpretive humility we established early on now finds practical application. As you notice material details (like roof tiles described in Chapter 6), or encounter performance moments layered with unpredictable combinations (as in Chapter 7), you build confidence as a reader ready for subtlety and surprise. These skills will serve you as we turn to regional diversity (Chapter 9), where no two towns blend their spiritual inheritances in quite the same way. Modern encounters with these traditions (Chapter 10) will challenge and reward the interpretive generosity you've cultivated here. Approach each site, ritual, or remixed festival with curiosity, patience, and the knowledge that blended paths often carry wisdom unavailable anywhere else (Khan Academy, 2018; 2023).

Chapter 8: Blended Paths: Syncretism, Doctrine, and Local Practice

## Bringing It All Together

Throughout this chapter, we've traveled through the layered history of how Japanese spiritual life wove Shinto and Buddhist traditions together. We saw how temples, shrines, rituals, and stories blended into everyday routines, creating a world where people didn't pause to separate what belonged to kami or buddhas—they simply cared for both. Even as official policies tried to draw sharp lines and redefine what counted as pure tradition, local communities found their own ways to hold onto blending and adaptation. Family rituals, seasonal festivals, and even small gestures at home kept old connections alive. Rather than breaking under pressure, these practices shifted shape to fit new rules while carrying deep meaning for each generation.

What stands out is how much creativity and warmth runs through the fabric of daily devotion. Households have adapted with gentle persistence, mixing prayers, objects, and folk wisdom to meet their unique needs. Folktales, memories, and practical choices all helped preserve the spirit of Shinbutsu Shugo, reminding us that lived experience is rarely neat or tidy. The real story is not about pure boundaries but about flexibility—how people made space for comfort and connection across traditions. As we move forward, remembering this adaptability will help us read rituals, sites, and stories with more openness and respect, honoring the many ways community and heritage continue to stitch meaning into everyday life.

# Chapter 9: Local Worlds: Regions, Crafts, and Story-Places

When people try to understand Japanese spirituality, they often expect one clear, simple story. Instead, they discover many different local worlds that don't fit together neatly. For example, coastal towns hold prayers hoping for safe returns from stormy seas, mountain villages turn to forests for mercy, and city neighborhoods carefully plan festivals around busy bus schedules. Each place carries its own unique rhythms and concerns shaped by the land and daily life. These aren't just quaint details but living traditions intertwined with the environment. The challenge is to appreciate these varied expressions without squeezing them into a single idea or putting them behind glass as artifacts.

This chapter invites you to see how identity, craft, and storytelling grow out of specific landscapes and ways of life. Understanding why a harbor's shifting winds matter or how a city dweller's lunch break shapes ritual opens new doors to experiencing kami traditions. We start by exploring how guardian spirits and stories take shape directly from the character of each place, revealing how people connect deeply to their local worlds through skill, belief, and shared memory.

# Regional Kami and Place-Based Identity

Spiritual life in Japan does not drift above landscapes; it grows from their soil, shorelines, and roads. While earlier chapters explored how kami inhabit natural features, here we see how specific landscapes generate distinct spiritual communities and rituals. Readers familiar with the presence of kami in rice paddies, home altars, or seasonal celebrations are ready for the next layer: seeing how a fisher's world, a mountain hamlet, a river crossing, or a pilgrimage trail each shape worship in their own image.

## Harbor Protectors

Fishing villages treat every launch into open water as an encounter with risk. In these places, sea guardians like Ebisu or Ryūjin (the dragon king) are honored at small shrines built near docks or harbors. Salt lies piled at altars to purify luck before departures, and boat prows are adorned with paper streamers (shide) that flutter like warning signals against unseen dangers. Before the first journey of the season, families gather to offer the year's first catch, pouring sake onto pier stones to thank the spirits and ask for smooth tides. The seasonal rites described in Chapter 4 take on different flavors depending on whether storms or droughts pose the greater threat—here, typhoon-season prayers act both as weather observation and ritual petition, blending meteorological care with spiritual respect. Stories about mysterious lights leading boats through fog are retold as safety instructions; they are guideposts passed down so that new sailors remember the tricky shoals and shifting sandbars. Over time, the dangerous reality of the sea becomes a shared knowledge base, supported by both practical tradition and spiritual reassurance. These place-shaped guardians naturally influence the skills and crafts that emerge from the same landscapes—a connection we'll explore in detail next.

**Forest Keepers**

Upland settlements organize their lives around ancient groves and hillside shrines dedicated to yamano-kami (mountain deities). Here, sacred forests serve not just as holy ground but also as watershed buffers and wildlife corridors. Families maintain clearings for periodic ceremonies where fresh water is offered at spring-fed basins, and wood from fallen limbs is carved for use in making kamidana, or household altars. Watching animal messengers—like deer, whose sudden appearance often marks the coming change from dry to rainy season—serves as both environmental awareness and spiritual communication. Bird migrations announce planting times, blurring the line between agricultural planning and reverence. Tree-blessing rituals double as acts of resource management, setting limits on which saplings can be cut and which must stay to hold slopes against landslides. Woodworking traditions are born from this world: each carved amulet or spoon carries the memory of careful observation and seasonal gratitude, foreshadowing the craft practices shaped by these upland realities, soon to be discussed.

## Bridge Watchers

Bridges demand special attention, both as feats of engineering and sites of risk. Communities raise stone markers and guardian figures—often foxes or sword-bearing statues—at either end. Walking children bow or touch the marker to acknowledge the local spirit believed to shield travelers from harm. Flood season brings extra offerings: coins pressed into crevices or straw sandals tied to rails, meant to keep feet steady across slippery planks. Legends warn of mischief-making spirits who might demand a toll or cause night accidents; in telling these tales, elders teach their neighbors where footing turns treacherous after rain or when mists rise thick over the river. Wayside signs and boundary posts double as behavioral cues, reminding passersby to mind their step and show respect. Maintaining these customs helps keep the memory of old floods alive, anchoring the village's relationship to the bridge as living infrastructure.

## Legend Trails

Travel routes become repositories where story and terrain weave together. Stone pillars with carved kanji retell episodes from famous pilgrim journeys or heroic rescues; their placement is carefully chosen to match story milestones with topographical features. A group of children walking with their teacher might stop at a mossy boulder engraved with poems, practicing both reading and remembering local legends. Story-stones and wooden posts are wayfinding tools, but they are also invitations to recall old wisdom about safe rest stops or hidden springs. Each festival that retraces a legendary route works like a communal act of memory refreshment, calling everyone out to walk the land and practice narrative literacy face-to-face. Elders lead hikes so no one forgets the stories tied to certain bends in the road, preventing names and histories from fading as years pass.

Daily work and devotion spiral out from these landscapes, shaping not only how people pray but what they make and how they pass on skill. Boatbuilding techniques, net-weaving patterns, amulet carving, and even the design of bridges all carry traces of their region's guardians and the environmental needs they answer. From the salt-sprinkled harbors to hillside cedar groves and the mnemonic stones along highland trails, the contours of place press meaning into every action. This interplay of environment, spirit, and handwork flows directly into the next section, where we discover how craftspeople inherit not just artisan techniques, but entire ways of seeing and honoring the world their ancestors shaped.

## Craft Lineages and Sacred Skill

The landscapes that give rise to harbor protectors and forest keepers also shape the hands that work within them. When a potter digs clay from a riverbank where spirits are said to dwell, or when a carpenter fells trees in groves watched by mountain kami, they create objects that carry the story of place as much as the story of skill. Local tools become more than implements; each chisel or plane carries marks of use, names of former hands, and sometimes a date inscribed along the handle. In one lacquer workshop, an old plane sits on the altar shelf, its blade bearing the faint outline of a temple beam it once helped smooth. Such items teach apprentices to see implements as living vessels of memory, not just instruments for shaping wood or clay.

Tools in these settings often travel through generations, handed down with stories attached—who first sharpened the blade, which roof tile it last shaped, what mishap left the nick on its edge. Artisans recount these stories during annual ceremonies, such as the first-sharpening in spring or the winter oiling of blades. Each event draws attention to patience, restraint, and the limits set by both human and material endurance. These routines are practical—preventing rust, preserving keenness—but they weave mentorship and respect into every motion. Apprentices learn there is gratitude in wiping a blade or gently storing a brush after work. These habits, simple at first glance, reveal the workshop's rhythm, where care for tools becomes a way to honor those who came before (Brandt, 2007).

Within many workshops, kamidana shelf-altars hold rice, salt, water, and the smoke of incense. Placed high above the busiest benches, these altars mark the boundaries between daily routine and sacred space. Offerings rest on clean white paper or in small dishes, refreshed every morning before tools touch timber or clay. The air around the altar is still, even when saws and hammers echo elsewhere. Here, prayers for safety feel sensible—fire, steel, and flying splinters make real dangers—and norito invocations set intentions for focus and vigilance. On some shelves, artisans pin handwritten notes describing near-miss accidents, reminders that ritual accompanies readiness. No one mistakes ritual for superstition; instead, it partners the checklist, anchoring attention before risky work begins.

Material selection brings another form of attentiveness. Woodworkers judge grain and age before cutting, knowing that felling too early—or at the wrong moon phase—weakens a beam or bowl. Potters gather clay from river bends, testing handfuls for sound, scent, and texture; some regions name their clays like dialects, proud of differences in color and strength. Even folded metal in blades speaks of minerals drawn from regional mountains. Before large projects, craft families offer grains or sake at the grove edge, asking permission and forgiveness for taking what they need. Offcuts and shavings rarely go to waste; instead, they become fuel, patchwork repairs, or tiny offerings beside shrines. These small gestures express a continuing conversation with land and community. Material ethics rests on the understanding that every resource carries a story and a debt (Marra, 1999).

Finished works circle back to their origins through gifts to shrines and temples. Bowls fired from the season's first batch, new knives, or lengths of cloth find places on altar steps, often presented with words naming the teachers, materials, and dreams sewn into each piece. Some communities gather once a year to repair or ornament shrine buildings, with roof tiles pressed by familiar hands or lanterns painted by local children under an elder's eye. Votive plaques hang nearby, painted not only with wishes but with images of brushes, chisels, and working hands, each panel turning private workshop hours into public story. Through these acts, materials gathered from rivers and woods return transformed, closing a quiet loop of care and gratitude (Kondo, 1990).

While craft lineages root skill in place, pilgrimage paths spread and refresh that knowledge across regions. Walking artisans meet others, share techniques, and leave traces of their own traditions wherever they stay. The journey itself becomes part of the lineage—a moving thread stitching together sacred skill, landscape, and story.

## Pilgrimage Paths and Learning by Walking

Just as artisans inscribe their legacy into tools and workshops, so pilgrims stamp their presence and learning into pages and pathways. In Japan, groups and individuals take up old routes that thread mountains, forests, and coastlines. These journeys echo the spirit of those who make and use sacred objects— every footstep is an act of making, a way of weaving one's own memory into the land (Reader, 2005). Rosaries, walking sticks, or talismans picked up along these routes become both tool and record, holding stories like heirloom chisels or weaving looms in village homes.

Pilgrims often collect stamps in dedicated booklets called goshuin-cho. "Goshuin"—meaning "honorable red stamp"— serves as proof of having visited temples or shrines along the way. Each stamp is brushed by hand, paired with calligraphy, and sometimes decorated with motifs like cranes, waves, or torii gates. These marks don't just log sites; they store sensations: the tremor in your hand after a strenuous climb, the scent of cedar mingling with wet ink, the cheer from sharing completed pages around a hostel table. Regional differences surface in shape, color, and drawing style, telling what matters locally and carrying echoes of place-based crafts. Swapping stamp books becomes a kind of conversation, breaking ice between travelers and linking memories to the present moment (Ambros, 2016).

Guides appear on these paths in many forms. Some are formally trained, while others are locals whose knowledge flows from everyday life—elderly women who know every bend in the road, teenagers explaining how the weather shapes what grows where. The best guides do not just recite facts but open doors to layered worlds. Imagine one stopping the group at a sudden curve: "This path bends here because the mountain once slid down after a typhoon." Or another pointing out moss on fence posts, naming it by its unique color, hinting at microclimates you'd miss if you hurried by. Good guides encourage travelers to slow down, look for tiny details in trail ruts or faded wooden signs, and ask questions about what puzzles or delights them. Writing these small discoveries in a notebook can turn each walk into a living archive (Reader, 2005).

Hostels and traditional inns line pilgrimage roads, sometimes centuries old themselves. More than places to rest, they are communal archives. Walls hold photos of past walkers, battered staffs lean beside umbrellas, and guestbooks fill with sketches, notes about rainstorms, or tips about nearby springs. Conversations with hosts reveal secret viewpoints, hard times, and stories handed down—sometimes patched together just like the roofs overhead. Rooms may display shared objects: coins left for luck, prayer beads, festival posters. When guests gather to share meals, their talk layers new meaning onto familiar rooms, like apprentices swapping the best ways to mend a split handle or polish a shrine bell. For anyone passing through, time spent writing or sketching here adds another page to the place itself (Ambros, 2016).

Seasons change what the path teaches. Spring brings petals underfoot, fresh water in streams, and the first mountain vegetables cooked at dinner—a feeling of waking memory. Summer's buzz urges early starts, with heat making shade precious. Autumn drapes trails in red and gold, a reminder of cycles ending and beginning. Winter hushes everything, leaving snowy silence and slow fireside conversations with innkeepers. The foods on offer, lanterns strung across open fields, even the mud or dryness of the path—all color the lessons taken home in journals and stamp books. Just as seasonal shifts set the pace for farm work or festivals back in hamlets, walking at different times of year opens up new ways of seeing and recording (Reader, 2005; Ambros, 2016).

Throughout this book, attention and gratitude have turned ordinary acts into sources of living memory. Whether shaping wood in a workshop or collecting stamps on a mountain pass, learning takes root in motion and repetition as much as stillness. Like crafting a blade or altar, the act of walking calls for patience and attention to detail, encouraging each person to tune senses, notice change, and treasure small interactions. This layering of memory prefigures what we'll encounter in city shrines next. As we'll see in city shrines, the urge to pause, notice, and record never truly vanishes. This way of learning endures, even as city-dwellers adapt old routines to new schedules and landscapes (Reader, 2005; Ambros, 2016).

## Urban Shrines and Modern Rhythms

Step into a crowded Tokyo intersection and notice how walking patterns feel patterned, even in the hurry. Every commuter, with checked steps or a glance upward, echoes the pilgrim's attentive journey—once laid out along ancient mountain routes, now repeated between skyscrapers and train platforms. The city tightens these slow rituals of place-learning into brief moments: crossing under a torii on the way to work, pausing by mossy stone at lunchtime, tracing familiar streets where the sacred returns as memory and marker.

Move past looping horns and traffic signals; find a patch of green behind an office block. These pocket groves, chinju-no-mori in miniature, draw breath for the neighborhood. Camphor and zelkova trees filter early sunlight while passengers wait at bus stops nearby. Step under the canopy and traffic noise softens, cool air gathering around stone basins where water glints. Lanterns throw shadow-shapes over damp moss; incense traces lift above planted roots. Even a momentary pause in such a grove refreshes attention, offering a sensory shelter. These microclimates are lively, home to nesting birds and pollinating bees—a practical ecology supporting ritual atmosphere (Nelson, 2013). This is not mere landscaping; it is a living threshold, scaling forest experience for the city block. Look for layered plantings, water bowls crusted with lichen, and paths flowing toward a single altar. These elements invite the body to recognize difference, shifting from outward rush to inward arrival.

Workers slip free from elevators and meetings, drawn by bells that sound soft and bright. Weekday shrine visits fit the tempo of urban life—five minutes snatched from lunch or evening commutes. Rinse hands at the stone basin, toss a coin into the offertory box, bow twice and clap, then ring the bell for the kami's attention. Where earlier villages prayed for rain or harvest, city dwellers offer petitions for project pitches, child health, or peaceful negotiations. A small noticeboard changes each month, displaying kanji for virtues—perseverance in

Chapter 9: Local Worlds: Regions, Crafts, and Story-Places

June, gratitude in November—teaching recurring lessons alongside repeated gestures. One visit blends into the next, a curriculum of noticing and intention set against office bustle (Reader & Tanabe, 1998). Short rituals here do not shrink deeper meaning; instead, they preserve continuity by adapting purpose and pace. The same care animates these five-minute devotions as dawn prayers along rural pilgrimage trails.

Neighborhoods knit themselves together through habit and ritual movement. Schoolchildren pass guardian fox statues on safe-walk routes, parents teaching them to bow before crossing the street. Commuter lines thread past small shrines tucked near station exits; some take quick detours to bow or leave flowers, seamlessly integrating devotion into their routine. Markets spring up beside courtyards, traders arranging seasonal fruit and sweets on offering trays before opening stalls. Recall how Chapter 6 traced the shaping power of thresholds—torii archways, shimenawa ropes—and how Chapter 4 followed the pulse of festival days. The same attention to thresholds reappears here in compressed form, guiding motion and gathering people into shared space. Urban places do not flatten tradition; they braid it into daily rounds, so the act of passing through becomes both transit and transformation.

Festivals bring these rhythms into full view, threading old intentions through new logistics. Parade planners coordinate float heights with trolley wires and bus schedules, mapping pauses at signal crossings and stroller stations. Volunteer crews pivot from collecting trash to guiding lost visitors, turning civic tasks into acts of hospitality. Event announcements ripple through local apps, splitting crowds across time slots to keep participation safe yet collective. Temporary lanterns hang from eaves and doorways, lighting routes through makeshift corridors of food stalls. These adaptations answer the squeeze of modern infrastructure without shedding ritual meaning (Hardacre, 2017). Creative problem-solving keeps festival processions connected to ancestral patterns, even as city blocks rearrange the path.

Across shoreline villages, mountain paths, and city intersections, a through-line remains: places teach by inviting repeated attention, reflection, and participation. Whether stepping beneath trees by a busy platform or finding shade beside an altar on the way to lunch, the encounter with kami persists as active relationship rather than static display. Each adaptation ties city rhythm to older roots, readying the ground for new expressions that will surface in the chapters ahead (Nelson, 2013; Reader & Tanabe, 1998; Hardacre, 2017).

## Bringing It All Together

Throughout this chapter, we've seen how searching for a single story of Japanese spirituality often misses the many living worlds that thrive in local places. Coastal towns pray to sea guardians for safe journeys, mountain villages honor forest spirits while protecting their slopes, and city neighborhoods fold old rituals into everyday routines like lunch breaks or festival planning. Each place shapes its own identity through a mix of challenges, skills, and stories—and these differences matter. By looking closely at how people relate to their surroundings, we find that spiritual practice is always grounded in daily life, not floating above it.

Understanding local kami traditions means paying attention to the details—why a bridge has two fox statues, how children learn legends on the walk to school, or what a bowl of salt beside a harbor shrine means before a storm. None of these practices fit into one neat slogan; instead, they invite us to read the land, listen to its people, and notice how story, skill, and place come together. This way of seeing asks us to respect each region's unique rhythm and recognize that meaning grows from lived experience. As we move ahead, remembering these lessons will help us appreciate both the diversity and creativity found in every landscape touched by kami traditions.

# Chapter 10: Continuity and Change: Modern Encounters with the Sacred

Imagine a child in the year 2035 strolling through a quiet Tokyo neighborhood where ancient camphor trees form cool pockets of shade, lowering the street temperature by several degrees. Around these trees, invisible sensors quietly monitor and protect their roots from being trampled, while small plaques invite passersby to listen to seasonal prayers, shared in the familiar voices of local elders. Just down the street, an after-school club breathes new life into old folktales, turning stories of river spirits and tips for weathering storms into short films that spark imagination and respect. Meanwhile, a neighborhood map app overlays historic shrine groves onto the city's green corridors, guiding walkers on weekend journeys that weave past and present together.

This glimpse into a near future may seem like daydreaming, but it shows what can happen when cultural heritage and environmental care walk hand in hand. To understand how communities might nurture such harmony, we start with the sacred groves already living and breathing in our world—places cared for by people who bring nature and tradition into daily life. These groves offer lessons about tending both roots and stories, showing us how respect for the past can grow alongside new ways of connecting with the sacred amidst modern change.

## Preservation, Ecology, and Sacred Groves

The sacred groves you've encountered throughout this book—marked by shimenawa, stewarded by local communities—face new pressures and possibilities today. Earlier chapters traced these living sanctuaries from ancient shrine landscapes (see Chapter 2) to marker stones at rural thresholds (Chapter 6) and regional adaptations in mountain and coastal zones (Chapter 9). Now, these spaces invite a different kind of attention: one that centers not only on reverence, but on active participation, ecological care, and the stories we carry forward. Each grove is a meeting place where spiritual tradition and environmental stewardship connect, shaping daily life and offering guidance for how engagement can continue in changing times.

A single tree, whether a monumental sugi or a modest plum at the edge of a shrine precinct, carries generations of memory. Tree stewardship begins with detailed documentation—a task as simple as a handwritten logbook or as accessible as phone photos uploaded each season. In Kamakura's Tsurugaoka Hachimangū, one 400-year-old camphor has a record tracing the family who first knotted its protective rope, now maintained by children who photograph its budding leaves each spring equinox. Mixed-age replanting ensures resilience:

in one community, grandmother cedars form the high canopy while saplings twenty years old already anchor lantern offerings. Citizen monitoring brings these practices into many hands; a solstice photo snapped by a grandchild becomes both family ritual and a data point for arborists tracking health across decades. This blend of personal and scientific archive turns everyday encounters with trees into preservation work anyone can join.

Tree care extends outward, connecting the grove's principles to city streets and green corridors. Urban planning translates respect for ancient trees into new forms. A morning walker in Setagaya follows maple shade from her apartment to a riverside shrine, pausing in pocket parks where sparrows and white-eyes gather—these routes mimic pilgrimage, showing how past and present flow together. City engineers use permeable paving near sacred sites; raindrops sink quietly into the ground, cooling the air and restoring rhythms familiar to earlier generations. Setback zones create acoustic pockets—cross the threshold and hear your own footsteps, shielded by tall grass and rooted silence. Developers who preserve mature groves receive density bonuses, part of incentive programs that channel funds back into seasonal maintenance and neighborhood events. In this way, the protective logic of shrine forests shapes the lived texture of entire neighborhoods, not just sacred precincts.

Community memory grows alongside ecological knowledge. Citizen archivists participate in seasonal photo walks, captioning images like 'First plum blossoms, northwest corner, earlier than last year.' Oral history days invite elders to share what they know: a shrine carpenter explains the grain direction of torii beams during repair, while a festival drummer recalls the rhythm shift required as the mikoshi rounds the final bend. Volunteers contribute to digital maps, marking veteran stumps, water springs, and animal tracks, so that young plantings maintain continuity with invisible histories beneath the soil. These collective records become practical tools and living stories, securing the link between biodiversity and local heritage. This fusion of ecological science and cultural memory exemplifies the living traditions we've traced from village shrines to urban neighborhoods, showing how reverence adapts without losing its core.

Challenges brought by climate change, urbanization, and aging trees call for attentive and creative responses. Communities prepare windthrow protocols: when a typhoon snaps sacred trunks, pre-selected arborists and neighbors mobilize within hours, salvaging limbs for ritual reuse and stabilizing soils with woven straw mats. Lightning rods and fungal monitoring offer quiet protection, reminders of care rather than intrusion. When an ancient tree must come down, replacement acknowledges natural cycles—interpretive signs explain that pruning or new planting secures vitality, not erasure. Adaptation here is guardianship; to sustain a grove is to accept change while preserving continuity. The documentation practices and community networks sustaining these groves also shape how their stories—and the values they embody—reach new audiences through contemporary media and education.

## Folklore in Media and Education

Sacred groves and stones root memory in place, but stories let values travel farther—into city apartments, distant classrooms, and late-night screens. Where trees cannot walk, tales cross boundaries, weaving a living fabric that can reach listeners long after the festival ends or after a shrine's wall is lost to time. Modern media and education become vessels for these stories, carrying tradition beyond physical locales and into hearts and minds across generations.

Retelling old myths for today's readers means more than repeating what came before. Contemporary authors reshape stories so they speak with fresh voices, sometimes shifting perspective to include those once left in the margins. When creators tell a river spirit's story from the spirit's own view, as in one recent children's book, pollution appears not as an abstract threat but as a wound felt—clouded water, silenced laughter, tangled debris stifling movement. The narrative then follows the spirit's slow recovery as local families organize cleanups, blending folktale with ecological care. This approach keeps the core themes of reciprocity and consequence alive while aligning them with environmental stewardship (Tanaka, 2020). More writers now include transparent afterwords or content notes: maps tracing the tale's regional roots, lists of sources used, explanations of choices made. These additions model respect and give educators, parents, and lifelong

## Chapter 10: Continuity and Change: Modern Encounters with the Sacred

learners tools to ask careful questions: Whose voice speaks here? Which traditions shape this retelling? What gets added, and what remains?

When stories move to the screen, filmmakers translate invisible cues of sacred presence into visual and sound language that viewers can feel. Animation often signals threshold crossings—the moment between everyday and holy—by washing colors towards gray as characters near torii gates, then letting hues bloom after stepping through. Sound slows down too: footsteps on gravel, breath in cold air, the hush before a bell rings. Directors linger on details that might be passed over—a tuft of bent grass by a path, shide (zigzag paper streamers) fluttering on a stormy morning—inviting a viewer's gaze to rest with intention. Character designs echo mask traditions; bold outlines, patterned kimonos, and simple faces remind us of the archetypes—guardian, trickster, ancestor—who once danced at crossroads or shrine festivals. In one striking montage, a caretaker sweeps his threshold through the year: cherry petals scatter for spring, cicadas hum in midsummer, red leaves drift in autumn, snow muffles sound in winter. No one explains why he bows before starting work, but the camera tells us through quiet repetition. When watching such scenes, you might notice how rhythm shifts at boundaries, how colors, silence, and costume hint at role, or how editing ties daily acts to seasonal change (Suzuki, 2018).

Museum exhibitions also play an active part in sharing folk spirituality, moving beyond static glass cases. The most engaging displays create sensory worlds: headsets bring in wind through cedars, distant bells, soft crunches of gravel, layered with taiko drumming or festival chants. Instead of presenting ritual objects as relics, curators rotate cases so a rice-offering bowl might appear with different backgrounds—one week as part of a planting petition, another as a harvest celebration, later beside ghostly lanterns for ancestral remembrance. Labels name not just the deity or object, but the human lives involved: the village metalworker who cast a bell, the families who ring it each New Year. During a museum visit, slipping on a headset transports a visitor to festival grounds even as she stands among display lights. Reading a label, she learns about the people who stewarded the artifact, the changes in its meaning through seasons, and the cycles connecting community to spirit. Visitors can start asking: What sounds, scents, and images help me understand context? Who crafted, carried, cleaned these objects? How does one item carry many meanings, depending on when and where it appears? (Nakayama & Sato, 2019)

Educators have found lively ways to draw folklore into civic and environmental lessons. Mapping activities invite students to trace streams on a local map, pairing each bend with legends of river spirits, then going out to adopt a stretch of creek for cleanup, blending imagination with responsibility. Teachers encourage role-play debates, assigning one child the voice of a mountain kami, another a logging company manager, a third a village elder—all practicing arguments about heritage, habitat, and livelihood. Reflective journals match weekly folktales with "noticing" entries—sounds on a morning walk, clouds above the schoolyard, shifts in scent as the seasons turn—to build gratitude and attention. These activities travel well: city or countryside, young or older students, adapted for any cultural background. Teachers and parents can ask themselves: How do these stories reflect our home landscape? What values or dilemmas come up? How can we practice noticing the world around us as part of learning? (Kobayashi, 2021)

The journey from myth to movie, showcase to schoolroom, reminds us that each choice—whose voice, what technique, which context—carries weight. Seeing how stories adapt and spread points toward deeper questions: Who should shape new versions? When does adaptation shade into distortion? How do we honor those who kept traditions alive? These are questions for the next pages, where ethical engagement takes center stage.

## Ethics of Appreciation, Not Appropriation

The creative retellings and educational innovations we just explored invite us to feel inspired—ready to share, adapt, or honor traditions that move us. At the same time, these acts carry the risk of misrepresentation if not approached with care. This next part offers practical steps for staying accountable as we engage with Japanese kami traditions and folk spirituality beyond observation, whether in art, education, travel, or daily practice.

Giving credit is more than a footnote; it's how we keep stories rooted in real communities and lineages. When sharing a story about kitsune, for example, say where you found it—"as collected by Yanagita Kunio in Tōno Monogatari (1910) from storytellers in Iwate Prefecture"—instead of simply labeling it "a Japanese folktale." This detail isn't about showing off scholarly chops but rather maintaining threads between a living story and the people who carry it. Using regional names like "Inari-sama" instead of only "kami" helps protect community identity and respects local voices, reminding us there is no generic Japan. If you give a talk or post online, suggest further reading drawn from works by Japanese scholars or shrine communities, not just English-language introductions—this lets listeners find their own way back to authentic sources. These habits counteract the kind of generalization and erasure that fuels appropriation, keeping appreciation alive and connected (*How to Avoid Cultural Appropriation & Promote Cultural Awareness Instead - Commisceo Global*, 2017).

Listening before using sacred practices or knowledge enriches your understanding and builds trust. Imagine planning a visit to a small mountain shrine. Before photographing, ask staff or caretakers if photos are permitted, since many sites restrict images to preserve sanctity. Preparing an educational workshop? Email a cultural center ahead of time to check what stories or crafts are okay to share. Recording festival music for your own project? Ask organizers for permission, and offer compensation if requested. Paying for expertise or donating to preservation funds acknowledges both spiritual and intellectual labor. Sometimes you'll hear "no," or learn that certain rituals or objects are not meant to be shared outside their original circle. Accepting this answer can feel hard, yet it's a mark of respect—for yourself, the tradition, and its guardians. This consultative approach becomes the foundation for recognizing the sacred in everyday life and creating new relationships rooted in trust and reciprocity (*How to Avoid Cultural Appropriation & Promote Cultural Awareness Instead - Commisceo Global*, 2017; Legault & Bleau, 2025).

Sharing what you've learned calls for humility. Instead of presenting stories or rituals as universal truths—"the Japanese believe…"—set the stage honestly: "In one version I encountered…" or "Some communities tell it this way…" These phrases both honor variation and signal your own learning journey. If you're invited to teach or interpret, pause to reflect on your experience level. Turning down requests to lead ceremonies or sell spiritual items you're not qualified for upholds both the tradition and your own integrity. Direct those interested to community-led events or resources whenever possible. When you do share, disclose your standpoint—outsider, learner, visitor—so others know where your perspective comes from. Humility doesn't mean holding back all curiosity or conversation. Instead, it means making space for the voices closest to the source, letting their authority guide your interpretation (Legault & Bleau, 2025).

Support for tradition bearers is most powerful when it meets real needs. Buying a locally crafted charm from a shrine shop supports those responsible for sacred spaces. Donations to forest restoration efforts or funding a roof repair help ensure that continuity isn't just a matter of words. Purchasing books directly from small Japanese presses or supporting artist collaborations brings resources into the community, not just to intermediaries. On top of these options, volunteering—whether by joining a shrine cleanup, helping translate educational materials, or offering skills requested by the custodians themselves—aligns your help with actual community priorities. It matters that support does not become transactional; contributing money or effort does not entitle you to use restricted practices. True appreciation means joining in the care and continuity of what moves you, not collecting pieces for personal gain (*How to Avoid Cultural Appropriation & Promote Cultural Awareness Instead - Commisceo Global*, 2017; Legault & Bleau, 2025).

Throughout this book, we've emphasized that respectful engagement grows from ongoing humility and care—not expert status or flawless behavior. The thoughtful guardrails above set the stage for building practices and perceptions shaped by reflection, which the next section will explore in more depth.

## Reading the Sacred Today: A Reflective Framework

Having established boundaries for respectful engagement with traditions that are not our own, we can now turn to practices that deepen personal perception and care in daily life. The question shifts from what to refrain from, to how we

## Chapter 10: Continuity and Change: Modern Encounters with the Sacred

might act—how to cultivate sacred awareness amid the ordinary, using the tools of attention, gratitude, place knowledge, and humility. Each of these grows from values found in kami traditions yet adapts them as open invitations for anyone seeking meaning without appropriation (*Sacred Sites and Archaeology: Respect and Understanding - Loveland Archaeological Society*, 2024; *Sacred Spaces of Adopted Lands: Interacting Respectfully*, 2024).

Attention, as a practice, forms the root of all other ways of honoring the sacred. You don't need to mimic behavior at shrines or learn formal rituals to begin. Instead, this kind of attention asks you to become aware each time you cross a threshold—as when your hand touches the door handle coming home. There's a change in temperature, maybe a shift in light, perhaps even the smell of outdoors lingering on shoes in the entryway. Letting yourself pause in these moments lets the ordinary become something you notice anew. This is akin to what Chapter 6 described about torii gates—not just as symbols, but as reminders to reset focus and invite a sense of presence.

Another way to deepen attention comes by tracking patterns over time. Weekly notes on wind direction, the calls of birds at sunrise, or subtle changes in light from one season to the next draw you into relationship with your local environment. These observations echo the cyclical, responsive habits discussed in Chapter 4's seasonal practices—giving you a slow-growing knowledge of your place much like farmers learned planting cycles by watching and waiting through repetition. Try a seasonal photography walk: take one photo in the same spot each week, watching how rain, sun, shadows, and leaves mark the steady drift of impermanence. Over weeks and months, this simple practice becomes its own quiet meditation, not for sharing online, but as a personal record of change and return.

Gratitude then emerges as a relational skill, not an obligation. It means letting dependency show—the coolness of tap water on your fingers reminds you of rivers, reservoirs, pipes, and people. Whisper thanks, not as prayer or performance, but as naming the chain that brings resources into your hands. You might write a line in the margin of your notebook after a meal: "Rice from Yamagata, picked by someone's hands, cooked here." At the table, mentioning who grew the vegetables, which hillside they traveled from, or the story behind a favorite bowl makes the meal more than fuel—it becomes a web of stories and connections. This approach draws from the storytelling traditions we explored in Chapter 5, where language itself stitched together gratitude and memory—all while avoiding any gesture that feels imitative or out of place (*Sacred Spaces of Adopted Lands: Interacting Respectfully*, 2024).

Place literacy offers another thread for reading the sacred today. Learning the names of where you are—both the official ones and those spoken by elders or written in old stories—lets you see deeper layers in the landscape. Places contain memory, sometimes with histories of joy, sometimes bearing scars. Asking shopkeepers or neighbors about a crossroad's history, listening for old names, or noticing which corners flood in spring, helps reveal the many stories held by the places you pass each day. For instance, keeping track of the first swallows' arrival or mapping trees along your regular

## Chapter 10: Continuity and Change: Modern Encounters with the Sacred

commute are simple acts that change everyday travel into attentive fieldwork. These small studies teach us not just to see, but to ask whose stories are held here, connecting back to the regional diversity and placed-based practices in Chapter 9.

Humility guides each step, acting as a compass. It pushes us to ask, "What am I missing? Who belongs here as guide?" before assuming expertise or taking souvenirs. When you visit somewhere meaningful, try taking fewer photos and spending more time present. If you spot a feather or stone, consider leaving it in place. Quiet acts of care—picking up litter, straightening a marker, supporting local maintenance funds, or simply departing respectfully—become ways of giving rather than extracting. Reciprocity here isn't transactional. It acknowledges that your attention and presence are part of the site's story too, gently shifting the impact from taking to tending (*Sacred Sites and Archaeology: Respect and Understanding - Loveland Archaeological Society*, 2024).

Imagine applying these practices right where you live. Your neighborhood block—with its old ginkgo tree, the puddle that never dries, benches worn smooth by conversation, and stories told between neighbors—can become a layer of living heritage. You might map the houses sheltering the oldest residents, note seasonal bird migrations, learn the origin of a street's name, or linger at doorways as you come and go, letting small pauses become your own kind of ritual. Continuity, then, comes not from trying to preserve things unchanged, but from renewing relationships of care, story, and place across time. Every act of noticing, every word of thanks, every humble question sows possibility for new ways to read and honor the sacred—right where you stand.

## Bringing It All Together

Walking with the child through Tokyo's shaded streets, we catch a glimpse of how caring for trees and traditions can shape daily life. Old camphors offer cool refuge under their wide branches, while new technologies quietly protect roots and invite us to listen to voices from seasons past. Around the corner, stories transform in creative hands—children retell river myths, apps connect walkers to hidden histories, and everyday moments become reminders that nature and heritage thrive when tended side by side. This vision doesn't belong only to the future: it lives in each record-keeping notebook, every seasonal festival, and in the simple act of pausing beneath a familiar tree.

This chapter has shown that sacred groves are more than relics—they're living classrooms where people learn, remember, and adapt together. By blending memory with science, honoring both resilience and change, communities keep tradition alive while welcoming new ideas. Whether preserving mature trees, sharing stories old and new, or mapping out meaningful places, these practices strengthen the web between people and place. Looking at today's neighborhoods through this lens, we can see endless possibilities for small, caring actions—each one building towards a future where heritage and ecology walk in step.

# Conclusion

As you reach the final pages of this book, I invite you to pause and reflect on the true spirit behind our journey together. From the beginning, my hope has been to move beyond surface-level glimpses of Japanese spirituality and guide you into a living world—one woven from quiet gestures, family stories, sacred trees, and shimmering moments where daily life meets the unseen. Rather than offering easy answers or tidy definitions, we've explored how kami traditions pulse at the heart of Japanese culture: as embodied relationships with nature, ancestors, and community that continue to grow, adapt, and inspire. This book never set out to prescribe rituals or present folklore as museum pieces; instead, it asks you to see these traditions as invitations—open doors to empathy, wonder, and shared discovery.

Looking back across the chapters, a tapestry of meaning takes shape. You've seen how mountains, rivers, and groves are not just settings but partners in the unfolding life of a place—breathing memory, blessing, and caution into every season. Household altars and ancestral tablets became portals through which gratitude and remembrance travel, turning ordinary routines into powerful expressions of belonging. Through New Year thresholds, rice planting prayers, bean-scattering, and boisterous festivals, we uncovered how time itself becomes rich with the texture of care, generosity, and renewal. Animal tricksters and mountain spirits taught us that wisdom does not always look like solemn rule-keeping—it can arrive in laughter, in mistakes, in the simple act of trying again. Folklore did not just entertain; it offered blueprints for fairness, resilience, and connection.

Material symbols—torii gates, amulets, shimenawa ropes, and handfuls of salt—showed us how everyday objects become bridges between visible and invisible worlds. The language of ritual and gesture, whether in grand processions or humble threshold-sweeping, reminded us to notice what is easily missed: the subtle shifts in mood, the hush before an offering, the warmth of shared effort on festival days. As we delved into the layered exchanges of Shinto and Buddhism, we witnessed the beauty of mixing, adaptation, and gentle negotiation rather than rigid boundary-setting. Regional chapters revealed that no single definition holds all the richness: from bustling city shrines to windswept harbors, each community shapes tradition in its own image, ensuring diversity thrives alongside continuity.

What may linger most, though, is a new way of seeing. This journey offered more than information—it asked you to slow down, notice the thresholds in your own daily life, and recognize the power in repeating small acts of care and gratitude. We learned that spirituality in Japanese folk practice is rarely about doctrine or uniform belief. Instead, it's a living ethic: a conversation between people and place, past and present, self and neighbor. It's about letting boundaries be soft, holding space for mystery, and respecting both the silence and the song—the rules and the joyful exceptions. The deepest respect grows from stepping lightly, listening deeply, and accepting that real understanding is always unfinished, always expanding.

Your commitment to exploring these themes with patience and curiosity is something truly worth celebrating. Many people long for shortcuts or sing-song summaries, but you brought openness and perseverance, reading closely and allowing complexity to challenge and enrich your view. That persistence matters. Now, you stand in a rare place—not only more culturally literate, but more attuned to nuance, context, and the need for humility. If you choose to share what you've learned—whether in family conversations, creative projects, or classroom discussions—you do so with a deeper sense of responsibility and care. Your appreciation is now grounded in understanding, ready to support respectful dialogue rather than quick consumption.

The end of a book is really another kind of beginning. Perhaps you'll feel drawn to visit a local shrine or community garden, read folktales aloud with friends, or trace the map of your neighborhood looking for unsung traces of history and spirit. Maybe you'll join discussion groups, write reflective posts in online forums, or reach out to cultural centers to keep learning and connecting. These types of engagement don't require expert status or special permission—they begin with listening, asking good questions, and honoring what others have carried before you. Each step you take toward thoughtful participation helps preserve the ethics at the heart of Japanese folk spirituality: respect, continuity, and the joy of shared stewardship.

## Conclusion

As you carry these lessons forward, remember that the desire to "give back" should always be guided by humility. The best contributions—whether supporting a preservation project, volunteering, or simply crediting sources when you tell a story—are those made in partnership, not appropriation. Avoid falling into the trap of treating tradition as a personal toolkit or fashionable accessory. Let curiosity remain coupled with caution. When possible, amplify the voices of tradition bearers, seek out diverse perspectives, and recognize the limits of any outsider's knowledge. True stewardship means knowing when to offer help, when to step back, and when to listen for guidance beyond your own experience.

Most importantly, thank you—for your trust, your time, and your open-hearted engagement. Writing this book has been a labor of both love and responsibility, shaped by countless conversations, interviews, and afternoons spent listening in sacred spaces. My greatest wish is that you walk away with not just knowledge, but a feeling of kinship: with people whose lives may look different from yours, with generations who kept these traditions alive, and with the lands and stories that hold such enduring power. Please know that you are always welcome to return—to reread, to write, to ask questions, and to share in the ongoing conversation that is Japanese folk heritage. Together, may we keep building bridges of respect, memory, and possibility—so that old wisdom and new understanding can continue to meet and flourish, wherever the journey leads next.

# Reference List

(2023). Study.com. https://study.com/academy/lesson/what-is-cultural-syncretism-definition-examples-quiz.html

Ajayi, J. (2024). *Animals behaviour in Japanese. International Journal of Culture and Education.* Jan Vrba Publishing House. https://www.researchgate.net/publication/377809068_Animals_Behaviour_in_Japanese

*An Annotated Bibliography of Global and Non-Western Rhetorics: Sources for Comparative Rhetorical Studies – Present Tense.* (n.d.). https://www.presenttensejournal.org/bibliographies/an-annotated-bibliography-of-global-and-non-western-rhetorics-sources-for-comparative-rhetorical-studies/

Agoda Travel Guides. (2025, January 23). *Discover Japan's Obon Festival 2024: Summer Magic Awaits!* Agoda: See the World for Less; Agoda Travel Guides. https://www.agoda.com/travel-guides/japan/discover-japans-obon-festival-2024-summer-magic-awaits/

Banda, C. V., Banda, J. T., & Singini, T. (2024, September 1). *Preserving Cultural Heritage: A Community-Centric Approach to Safeguarding the Khulubvi Traditional Temple Malawi.* Heliyon; Elsevier BV. https://doi.org/10.1016/j.heliyon.2024.e37610

*Decoding the Traditional Japanese New Year Decorations.* (2024). Arigatotravel.com. https://arigatotravel.com/blog/japanese-new-year-decorations

*Explore the Fascinating Realm of Ancient History – Scripture Analysis.* (2025, May). Scriptureanalysis.com. https://www.scriptureanalysis.com/explore-the-fascinating-realm-of-ancient-history/

Fujiwara, S., & Miura, H. (2025, December 11). *Youth Culture and Religion in Twenty-First Century Japan.* Cambridge University Press EBooks; Cambridge University Press. https://doi.org/10.1017/9781009550239

Gede, A., Ahmad Munjin Nasih, None Sumarmi, Idris, N., & Kurniawan, B. (2024, January 1). *Local wisdom as a model of interfaith communication in creating religious harmony in Indonesia.* Social Sciences & Humanities Open; Elsevier BV. https://doi.org/10.1016/j.ssaho.2024.100827

*Harai | religious rite.* (n.d.). Encyclopedia Britannica. https://www.britannica.com/topic/harai

*How To Avoid Cultural Appropriation & Promote Cultural Awareness Instead - Commisceo Global.* (2017, June 7). Commisceo Global. https://commisceo-global.com/articles/how-to-avoid-cultural-appropriation-promote-cultural-awareness-instead/

Hori, I. (1975). *Shamanism in Japan.* Japanese Journal of Religious Studies; Nanzan University; JSTOR. https://doi.org/10.2307/30233086

Jann. (2022, July 31). *People, nature and the five elements in Japan*. Elemental Japan. https://elementaljapan.com/2022/07/31/people-nature-and-the-five-elements-in-japan/

Johnson, F. (2025). *Museum masks: Unmasking the stories, craftsmanship, and cultural significance of ancient and indigenous artifacts*. Wonderful Museums. Retrieved from https://www.wonderfulmuseums.com/museum/museum-masks/

*Japan's Obon festival: how family commemoration and ancestral worship shapes daily life*. (2022, August 12). TalkDeath. https://talkdeath.com/japans-obon-festival-how-family-commemoration-and-ancestral-worship-shapes-daily-life/

Jason. (2025, June 10). *Kitsune: Exploring the Mythology and Powers*. StorytellingDB. https://storytellingdb.com/kitsune-japanese-mythology/

Kumar, P. (2023). *Tracing connections: The genealogy method in anthropology*. BA Notes. Retrieved from https://banotes.org/anthropology-research-methods/genealogy-method-anthropology/

Khan Academy. (2018). *Syncretism*. Khan Academy. https://www.khanacademy.org/humanities/world-history/ancient-medieval/syncretism/a/syncretism-article

*Kamidana – David Chart's Blog*. (2021, January 29). Davidchart.com. https://www.davidchart.com/2011/01/01/kamidana/

*Localizing the Global: The Shakuhachi's Place in "American" Culture - ProQuest.* (2022). Proquest.com. https://search.proquest.com/openview/24bc807233e7645760b06349ed843422/1?pq-origsite=gscholar&cbl=18750&diss=y

Legault, G., & Bleau, D. (2025, January 7). *Indigenizing or Appropriating? Navigating the Boundaries of Institutional Decolonization.* Capitalism Nature Socialism; Taylor & Francis. https://doi.org/10.1080/10455752.2024.2445586

Montagu, J. (2017, June 20). *How Music and Instruments Began: A Brief Overview of the Origin and Entire Development of Music, from Its Earliest Stages.* Frontiers in Sociology. https://doi.org/10.3389/fsoc.2017.00008

McKinley, C. E. (2023, March 9). *"Prayer is universal": How integrative faith practices enable Indigenous peoples' persistence and resistance to transcend historical oppression.* Psychology of Religion and Spirituality. https://doi.org/10.1037/rel0000497

Ravitch, F. (n.d.). *BYU Law Review The Shinto Cases: Religion, Culture, or Both-The Japanese Supreme Court and Establishment of Religion Jurisprudence The Shinto Cases: Religion, Culture, or Both-The Japanese Supreme Court and Establishment of Religion Jurisprudence.* https://digitalcommons.law.byu.edu/cgi/viewcontent.cgi?article=2873&context=lawreview

Shizuka, S. (2023, November 2). *The Meiji Restoration and the Secularization of Buddhism.* Nippon.com. https://www.nippon.com/en/japan-topics/b09409/

Sustainability Directory. (2025, July 28). *Sacred Groves → Term. Lifestyle → Sustainability Directory.* https://lifestyle.sustainability-directory.com/term/sacred-groves/

*Sacred Spaces of Adopted Lands: Interacting Respectfully.* (2024, January 25). https://druidry.org/resources/sacred-spaces-of-adopted-lands-interacting-respectfully-with-native-sacred-sites

*Shinto, Nature and Ideology in Contemporary Japan: Making Sacred Forests 1474289932, 9781474289931.* (n.d.). Dokumen.pub. https://dokumen.pub/shinto-nature-and-ideology-in-contemporary-japan-making-sacred-forests-1474289932-9781474289931.html

*Shinto.* (n.d.). Ultimate Pop Culture Wiki. https://ultimatepopculture.fandom.com/wiki/Shinto

*Shinto Shrine Guide - Iconography, Objects, Superstitions in Japanese Shintoism.* (2010). Onmarkproductions.com. https://www.onmarkproductions.com/html/shrine-guide-2.shtml

Swancutt, K. (2019, June 25). *Animism.* Cambridge Encyclopedia of Anthropology. https://www.anthroencyclopedia.com/entry/animism

*Shinto: Kami, Nature Spirits & Ancestors | Asian Gods and Goddesses Class Notes*. (2025). Fiveable.me. https://fiveable.me/asian-gods-and-goddesses/unit-8

*Shinto & Shintoism Guidebook, Guide to Japanese Shinto Deities (Kami), Shrines, and Religious Concepts*. (n.d.). Www.onmarkproductions.com. https://www.onmarkproductions.com/html/shinto.shtml

*Sacred Sites and Archaeology: Respect and Understanding - Loveland Archaeological Society*. (2024, March 2). Loveland Archaeological Society. https://lovelandarchaeologicalsociety.com/sacred-sites-and-archaeology-respect-and-understanding/

*Setsubun*. (2016, January 30). Nippon.com. https://www.nippon.com/en/features/jg00013/

Team, T. J. S. (2022, January 12). *Ultimate Guide to Setsubun*. Japan Switch. https://japanswitch.com/ultimate-guide-to-setsubun/

*Tokyo Local Culture Guide: Traditions & Modern Customs*. (2025, November 4). Machupicchu.org. https://www.machupicchu.org/tokyo-local-culture-guide-traditions-modern-customs.htm

Wiysahnyuy, L. F., & Ngalim Banfegha Valentine. (2023, February 6). *Folktales as indigenous pedagogic tools for educating school children: A mixed methods study among the Nso of Cameroon*. Frontiers in Psychology; Frontiers Media. https://doi.org/10.3389/fpsyg.2023.1049691

Xavier, J. (2020, May 28). *Shinto Symbols: The Meanings of the Most Common Symbols Seen at Japanese Shinto Shrines.* Www.tsunagujapan.com. https://www.tsunagujapan.com/shinto-symbols-meaning-and-history/

efelle creative. (2020). *Japanese Holidays 2020 | Summer Holiday Guide | Sugimoto Tea Company, Japanese Green Tea Maker Since 1946.* Sugimotousa.com. https://www.sugimotousa.com/blog/japanese-holidays-2020-summer-holiday-guide?srsltid=AfmBOoqa3en8bQiEG1Qvb4WCx4OEmjSYqRx-q4bR7Lfs4jnvkqFsocDR

www.ingramcontent.com/pod-product-compliance
Lightning Source LLC
Chambersburg PA
CBHW050637160426
43194CB00010B/1703